Business Etiquette and Professionalism

M. Kay duPont,
Certified Speaking Professional

CRISP PUBLICATIONS, INC.
Los Altos, California

Business Etiquette and Professionalism

M. Kay duPont,
Certified Speaking Professional

CREDITS
Editor: **Elaine Brett**
Design and Composition: **Interface Studio**
Cover Design: **Carol Harris**
Illustration: **Ralph Mapson**

Copyright © 1990 by Crisp Publications, Inc.
Printed in the United States of America

Crisp books are distributed in Canada by Reid Publishing, Ltd., P.O. Box 7267, Oakville, Ontario, Canada L6J 6L6.

In Australia by Career Builders, P.O. Box 1051, Springwood, Brisbane, Queensland, Australia 4127.

And in New Zealand by Career Builders, P.O. Box 571, Manurewa, New Zealand.

Library of Congress Catalog Card Number 89-81952
duPont, M. Kay
Business Etiquette and Professionalism
ISBN 1-56052-032-9

ABOUT THIS BOOK

BUSINESS ETIQUETTE AND PROFESSIONALISM is not like most books. It has a unique "self-paced" format that encourages a reader to become personally involved. Designed to be "read with a pencil," there are an abundance of exercises, activities, assessments and cases that invite participation. Good etiquette is good business!

The objective of this book is to teach the basics of business etiquette leading to the development of a personal action plan that will help a reader make some positive behavioral changes to improve the quality of his or her social awareness and manners.

BUSINESS ETIQUETTE AND PROFESSIONALISM (and the other self-improvement titles listed in the back of this book) can be used effectively in a number of ways. Here are some possibilities:

—**Individual Study.** Because the book is self-instructional, all that is needed is a quiet place, some time and a pencil. By completing the activities and exercises, a person should not only receive valuable feedback, but also practical ideas about steps for self-improvement.

—**Workshops and Seminars.** The book is ideal for reading prior to a workshop or seminar. With the basics in hand, the quality of the participation should improve. More time can be spent on concept extensions and applications during the program. The book can also be effective when a trainer distributes it at the beginning of a session, and leads participants through the contents.

—**Remote Location Training.** Copies can be sent to personnel who cannot easily attend training sessions to use for self-study.

—**Informal Study Groups.** Thanks to the format, brevity and low cost, this book is ideal for "brown-bag" or other informal group sessions.

There are other possibilities that depend on the objectives, program or ideas or the user. One thing for sure, even after it has been read, this book will serve you well as a ready reference and reminder about how to insure you understand and practice the principles of good business etiquette.

CONTENTS

iii

CONTENTS (Continued)

S E C T I O N

I

What Is
Business Etiquette?

ETIQUOTE

Etiquette is what you are doing and saying when people are looking and listening. What you are thinking is your business.

—Virginia Cary Hudson
O Ye Jigs & Juleps!

WHAT IS BUSINESS ETIQUETTE?

Good office manners may not be listed in your job description, but they certainly play a crucial part in your career. The ability to handle yourself properly today outweighs even your technical skills. If you know what to do, when to do it, and how to do it with grace and style, you'll have a competitive edge in your career. An October 1988 *USA Weekend* story emphasized that one of the themes for the 1990s is: "Good manners means good business." All the business experts agree.

Why is etiquette so important? Because people judge you and your company by what they see, and what they *believe* to be true. You are never really *you* to other people; you are only the you that they perceive you to be. If they perceive that you're even slightly uncultured and unrefined, your business may suffer. If people perceive you to be a knowledgeable, smooth professional, they'll want to do business with you.

If you questioned all the experts on business manners, each would probably give you a slightly different explanation of what constitutes good behavior in business. Acceptable etiquette even varies from place to place and from person to person. The codes of business conduct in Japan or China differ greatly from those in Alabama or California. Within the United States itself, what is acceptable in New York might be offensive in New Mexico. Even in your own city, an older person might be upset by behavior that would go unnoticed by a younger person. The titles *Mr.* and *Mrs.* or *Ma'am* and *Sir*, for example, annoy some people or seem stuffy, while other people *prefer* this formality. Some companies encourage the use of first names at all levels of employment, while others find this practice to be unforgivably familiar.

Even so, today's business etiquette is much simpler than a few years ago. Terms like *social graces, style, niceties, courtesy,* and *acceptable procedure* help to give us a sense of it. The 1988 *Webster's New World Dictionary* formally defines *etiquette* as "the forms, manners, and ceremonies established by convention as acceptable or required in social relations, in a profession, or in official life." Business etiquette, then, is the way professional businesspeople—no matter what their job title or type of business—conduct themselves around others.

Business etiquette relies on tradition, social expectations, and behavior standards. *Those* things are based on understanding, kindness, courtesy, efficiency, and common sense. What business etiquette boils down to is the *new* Golden Rule: *Do unto others as they would have you do unto them.*

THE ROLE OF GOOD MANNERS IN BUSINESS

As we become a more high-tech society, the need for a sensitive, personal touch in business increases. As John Naisbitt says in *Megatrends*, "Whenever new technology is introduced into society, there must be a counterbalancing human response." No matter how intelligent or accurate your computer is, you must still interact with other people.

When you use accepted etiquette, you're using the behaviors that encourage that human response; you're more likely to get positive results, earn cooperation and support, get commitments, gain clients, and keep peace. Those people you depend on in a pinch will usually come through for you. You are more likely to succeed when you put that something extra into your way of doing business.

Letitia Baldrige is one of the most respected etiquette experts in the U.S. She served in the Diplomatic Corps, and she spent three years as director of staff for Jacqueline Kennedy in the White House. In *Letitia Baldrige's Complete Guide to the New Manners for the 90s*, she says:

> Good manners are cost-effective. They increase the quality of life in the workplace, contribute to optimum employee morale, embellish the company image, and hence play a major role in generating profit. On the other hand, negative behavior, whether based on selfishness, carelessness, or ignorance, can cost a person a promotion, even a job.

A recent U.S. Office of Consumer Affairs' study revealed some of the costs of poor etiquette. The study showed that "up to 90% of unhappy customers never complain about discourtesy, and up to 91% will never again do business with the company that offended them. In addition, the average unhappy customer will tell the story to at least nine other people, and 13% of unhappy customers will tell more than twenty people."

As Letitia Baldrige comments, "A company becomes a company you want to do business with because of the people who work in it, so business etiquette has a very definite relationship to the bottom line."

When viewed in this light, business etiquette is more than which fork to use for salad, or how to smile nicely, or when to wear a tuxedo. Today's businesspeople must know how to walk into a room full of strangers and feel at ease. They need to be able to introduce themselves and others without feeling apprehensive. They should know when—and how—to make a telephone call to cheer or congratulate someone, and when a handwritten note is in order. They must know how to conduct themselves at company social functions and receptions, and understand the complexities of the business lunch.

In this book we're going to talk about common business situations and the etiquette that applies. We'll be talking about *American* etiquette; remember that other cultures have different customs. With our growing global economy, it's certainly not uncommon to be involved with people from all parts of the world. This requires a smooth stream of communication, free from social misunderstandings that may hinder the accomplishment of our business goals. We must learn to respect other cultures and to recognize the way they do business and socialize. For an excellent book on understanding cultural differences, read the Crisp Publications 50-minute book *Working Together* by Dr. George Simons that may be ordered using the form in the back of this book.

GOOD ETIQUETTE EQUALS GOOD BUSINESS

SOME ETIQUETTE BASICS

Holding Doors

Yesterday's etiquette dictated that a man had to back up and let a woman pass through the door first; a younger person had to do the same for an older person. But today's commonsense etiquette dictates that the person in the lead holds the door for the person in the rear. It's that simple. Of course, you junior executives might want to *arrange* it so you arrive at the door first!

If people of the same gender approach a door together, the one in the higher position or the one considerably older usually enters first, while the other person holds the door for them.

What about *revolving* doors? Why should the type of door make any difference? If the woman is in the lead, she enters first and pushes; the man follows and pushes. If the person in the rear wants to push a little harder to help out, that's great. The point is not who goes first, but that everyone gets through the doors easily.

Just remember that common sense rules. If someone is carrying an armful of files or packages, the other person takes the lead in all situations, regardless of sex or age.

One important thing has *not* changed: It's as bad to point out someone else's poor manners as to have poor manners yourself!

BUSINESS ETIQUETTE BASICS HAVE BEEN IMPORTANT FOR CENTURIES

Train Etiquette

What about the rule that men or younger people must give up their seats on a bus, train, or subway to women or older people? Not any more—unless the people are handicapped or pregnant. Of course, offering your seat is still a nice gesture.

Taxi Etiquette

Once a man would have relinquished his claim to a taxi for a woman, but no more. In cities like New York where you're lucky to get a cab in the first place, you're not likely to relinquish it to anyone. Most men still prefer to hold the door of a taxi for a female companion, but women needn't expect a taxi *driver* to jump out and hold the door. You may be waiting a very long time!

Automobile Etiquette

It's nice, but not mandatory, for a man to go around to the passenger side and assist a woman into the car when they travel together. It's especially appropriate when the car is locked. If someone *does* unlock your door from the outside, please be polite enough to unlock the driver's door from the inside! On a very busy street, however, it's acceptable (and good sense) for the driver to get into the car from the passenger side before the passenger does, if the car's seat design allows it.

Getting out of the car is another story. Some women find it embarrassing for men to come around and open their car doors. What does she do while she's waiting? If, however, the woman is dressed for a social event and might have trouble maneuvering her dress and wrap, then of course a man should help. If you're a woman with a man who *insists* on opening your door, good manners dictate that you allow him this tradition without a show of resentment.

It's still good manners for a man to walk a woman to her car in a dangerous area, or anywhere at night. Of course, it's smart friendship for a man to walk a *man* to his car as well! And women should always walk into parking lots in groups if possible.

SOME BASICS (Continued)

Elevator Etiquette

Common sense dictates that the people closest to the elevator doors get on first. If you want to be at the front when it's time to get out, go in and stand by the buttons, out of the way. Or go in last. When the elevator opens on your floor, leave. Don't stand around to see who else is leaving. If you're in the very front waiting for your floor, however, you show good manners if you move outside the doors to allow people to exit from the back. Consideration of the entire group should always come before formal etiquette to one person, especially in an elevator!

If you're using the escalator instead of the elevator, the man usually follows the woman. If you're using the stairs, the man usually follows the woman going up and precedes her going down.

Street Etiquette

What about the rule that a man has to walk on the street side of the curb? That's really an old one! It came into being during the days before paved streets, when mud was prevalent and garbage and waste were still being thrown out of open windows overhead. Men were supposed to be gallant enough to let *their* clothes get dirty. Today it's not feasible to walk along a busy street changing sides every few blocks just to make sure the man stays on the street side. Nor must a man offer his arm to a woman as they walk. If he is walking with two women, his place is on one side, but not necessarily on the outside.

EXERCISE

Take a moment to picture one or two people you see as real professionals—people you look up to. Write their names here and then describe their business etiquette. What do they *do* in business situations that make them appear professional? What do they *avoid* doing? List as many behaviors as you can before you go to Chapter 2.

(1) Name: _____

_____

(2) Name: _____

_____

What do they do?

(1) _____

_____

_____

_____

(2) _____

_____

_____

_____

Place a check by the behaviors *you* regularly use.

What do they *avoid* doing?

(1) _____

_____

_____

_____

(2) _____

_____

_____

_____

Put a check by the behaviors *you* intentionally avoid.

blank page 10

S E C T I O N

II

Principles of
Impeccable
Work Behavior

ETIQUOTE

If you would be happy for one hour, take a nap.
If you would be happy for a day, go fishing.
If you would be happy for a month, get married.
If you would be happy for a year, inherit a fortune.
If you would be happy for life, love your work.

—Chinese Proverb

blank page 12

PRINCIPLES OF IMPECCABLE WORK BEHAVIOR

Congratulations! You got the job! Whether you're a new permanent employee or one of America's 35 million contingent workers (temporaries, leased employees, independent contractors, and part-timers), you've just become the ''new kid on the block,'' and people are going to be watching you closely. It's easy to deal with your new coworkers' initial curiosity and, at the same time, establish yourself as a professional in your new position.

BASIC GUIDELINES

The guidelines in this chapter apply to *all* employees, not just newcomers. Many veteran workers also need to be occasionally reminded of these basic principles of business professionalism.

1. *Be careful with your appearance.* Dress within the parameters practiced at your company.

2. *Honor other people's territory.* See page 53 in Section V.

3. *Expand your knowledge.* According to a 1988 study by the U.S. Department of Labor and the American Society for Training and Development (ASTD), learning and knowing how to learn is the skill most needed by employees. Learning helps us be adaptable and flexible and is critical for dealing with organizational change and providing the flexibility to expand our jobs.

   Learn as much as you can about your job and your manager's job, and how they fit into the organizational structure. Find out what other departments do. Read the trade publications of your industry and profession. After you've read them, ask questions if you need to. Be the one that people turn to for expertise in your area.

4. *Honor your working hours.* Working nine to five doesn't mean that you *arrive* at nine and *leave* at five. It means you *work* from nine to five. Socializing at the coffeepot or eating breakfast at your desk is not working. Neither is saying goodnight at the elevator. Five minutes may not seem like much to you, but it may seem like stealing to your manager or CEO, especially in a small or very busy office. Ten minutes on a personal phone call is only a small part of an eight-hour day, but ten minutes a day equals fifty minutes a week—almost an hour of unproductive time.

   If you start getting ready to leave at 4:45, charge out of the office at 4:59, and go screeching out of the parking lot, you'll give the impression that you can't wait to leave—not a very professional attitude. If you cut short a telephone conversation with a customer because it's quitting time, you may lose the business. If you don't come to work because of mildly bad weather, you may find you're not as indispensable as you think.

BASIC GUIDELINES (Continued)

Honor your working hours. (Continued).
Skimping on your working hours not only displays bad manners, it also shows a lack of initiative, commitment and respect for your manager, your company, and your position. It says to others, "I simply work here; I don't have my heart in it." If you arrive at a meeting late, it says, "My time is more valuable than yours; you aren't important to me." Working your full hours (and more) shows dedication, and it's impossible for management to ignore. Those few extra minutes and that show of patience may make a big difference in the way you're considered for promotions or raises. Be honest. How many hours do you really work?

5. *Be friendly.* When you're new, you need people to help you with your new duties, explain procedures, or show you where to get information or materials you'll need. Make an extra effort to get along with everyone, but don't try *too* hard. Ask your new coworkers to have lunch with you; lunch is a great opportunity to get to know each other, and you can also ask questions and show that you'd like to help them if you can. Remember that offices work best when individual effort supports the team effort. Lunch can set the tone. And when someone new comes on board, go out of your way to invite *them* to lunch. Introduce them to your associates and coworkers and make them feel at home.

6. *Keep personal information to yourself.* Friendliness aside, don't let your life become the office soap opera. When someone asks, "How are you?" don't spill your guts. Some of that information could be used against you later. If you can't control your mood or your mouth, be quiet. The same advice goes, of course, for sticking your nose into others' personal business. Don't. Never discuss or question salary or any other confidential or personal information with coworkers.

7. *Be positive and supportive.* When your day isn't going the way you hoped it would, try to look at the positive side of things...and people. You'll be surprised how quickly you can turn a bad day into a good one. Believe in your coworkers and back them up in public. When your manager makes a decision, give your wholehearted support to it, at least in front of others. Make others look good at every opportunity. Managers, especially, need you to look, talk, write, and act like a positive, supportive representative. Your professionalism reflects on both your manager and your new organization.

8. *Keep an open mind.* Make informed judgments, avoid jumping to conclusions, evaluate what you see in addition to what you hear, and don't be a party to gossip. Establishing yourself as a professional means that you show respect for others.

9. *Follow through.* We all get a little tired, especially by late afternoon, but the job you tackle at 5:00 p.m. means as much as the one at 8:00 a.m. Cover every angle of a project, and don't wait to be reminded that you need to finish a project. Be accurate. Check and double-check to make sure things are going smoothly...the way you planned. Be realistic about how long an assignment will take, and let others know ahead of time if you anticipate a delay. Set deadlines and meet them.

10. *Communicate.* According to the ASTD study mentioned earlier, only job knowledge ranks above communication skills as a factor for workplace success. Keep people informed in a succinct and useful way. Everyone wants to know what's going on. Not every little detail of every day, but what is happening on major projects. Your coworkers want to know about the status of assignments. They want to know where you are when you're in, and how long you'll be gone when you're out. They want to know immediately about any problems or mistakes. Don't pester people or make them angry by wasting their time with the obvious or trivial, but don't let important matters get buried. Bring them to the right person's attention. Most of all, if a conflict arises or if someone makes a mistake, remember that everyone is human.

   Managers want you to go through the normal channels of communication. Don't go over their heads and don't bring things to them that don't concern them. If you want to disagree with them, do it tactfully, with a positive alternative and during a high point in the day.

11. *Listen.* Speaking and listening are twin skills in communication. Both sides must play a part for communication to occur, and you can learn best by listening to what others know. Ask questions. Hear how other people organize their ideas, how they bring up a new plan, how they respond to changes in procedures. Listen to the way they address those of higher rank. Listen for unspoken strengths and weaknesses. By caring about the way your co-workers feel, you can gain their loyalty and they'll be willing to contribute extra effort when you need it. Show that you are *interested*, not just *interesting*. By showing everyone that you want to learn from *their* knowledge and experience, you'll establish yourself as someone who wants to get the job done right. For more on listening, see Section V.

BASIC GUIDELINES (Continued)

12. *Solve your own problems.* When you do have to present a problem, bring possible solutions too. Don't complain about things that can't be changed, and don't blame others when you make a mistake. Excuses don't change the fact that something is late or incorrect. Accept responsibility when you've made a mistake and work harder to make sure it doesn't happen again. Learn to accept criticism gracefully—without defensiveness.

13. *Work hard.* Be ready and willing. Take on new responsibilities. Do more than others expect. Don't be content to do only what's expected of you or use the excuse that ''It's not my job.'' Look for areas in which you can do more and make yourself more valuable. Volunteer for special projects. Those who wait to be told what to do continue to be told what to do and their value seldom increases.

14. *Don't be in too big a hurry to advance.* Learn as much as you can in the job you have now. Think ahead. Plan. It's like growing up; no matter how eager you are, it takes a certain amount of time. Try to enjoy what you have while it's yours.

CLOSING DAY

If you don't have the job very long, keep your disappointment—or your extreme happiness—to yourself. Just be cordial and say your goodbyes quietly. Never badmouth the people who have put money in your pocket.

If someone else is leaving, respect that person's privacy as much as your own. Don't ask embarrassing questions or try to commiserate by demeaning the company or the person who handed down the bad news. But don't go out of your way to avoid this person either. Even if they resigned, and you can't understand why, respect their opinion. They're still the same people—they just chose not to work there any longer.

That doesn't mean that all your social activities with this person must come to an end, even if he or she is no longer part of the work crowd. This happened to my husband Jeff at his last corporate position. He had been a junior executive for a well-known conglomerate for several years. We had some close friends within the corporate circle, and were even asked to be at the hospital for the delivery of one couple's first child. When the company decided it didn't need Jeff's department anymore, everyone in the department was terminated. Since the conglomerate was unable to place Jeff in another position, he was retired (at the age of 35). We suddenly had the plague. None of our "friends" would talk to us and we were never invited back into that social circle. We also never saw that child again. Don't be guilty of inflicting shame on yourself or others just because a position didn't last.

Think about the last time you left a job. How professional was it?

*ALWAYS STRIVE TO LEAVE
ON A POSITIVE NOTE*

EXERCISE

Answer *true* or *false*. For those you answer false, what *is* the correct answer?

True	False	
☐	☐	1. When a new co-worker asks, ''Are you dating anyone right now?'' you should stalk off, saying, ''I don't think that's any of your business.''
☐	☐	2. You've been on the job a week and have noticed this good-looking co-worker down the hall. You should say something like, ''Hey, what's a good-looking person like you doing in a dump like this?''
☐	☐	3. When someone in your office does something nice for you that you didn't request, you should ask them why they did it.
☐	☐	4. It's perfectly all right to discuss your salary with your coworkers.
☐	☐	5. It's acceptable to come to work late as long as you don't go to lunch.
☐	☐	6. As a temporary employee, you don't have to be concerned about your professional image since you'll only be at the company a few days.
☐	☐	7. A speaker has greater responsibility than a listener in the communication process.
☐	☐	8. The more outgoing you are in the first few days of a new job, the more your coworkers will like you.
☐	☐	9. Your new manager will *always* be happy to answer questions and solve problems for you.
☐	☐	10. When you take a new or temporary job, it's the responsibility of the other employees to make sure you are happy and comfortable.

Answers on page 112

S E C T I O N

III

Meeting People

MEETING PEOPLE

You know what they say: A bad first impression is hard to overcome. Accurate or not, that first impression usually lasts. Whether you're a receptionist or a vice president, contact with you may be the only contact a person will ever have with your company. To them, you *are* the company. That's why you should see to it that every visitor to your office gets a cordial yet businesslike welcome.

> The way you greet others—not only by what you say, but by your body language—tells a lot about you. Meeting others in a pleasant way and showing sincere interest in them helps produce a favorable first impression.

When You're The Receptionist

Pretend you're the receptionist (or the primary person in a visitor reception area). A visitor comes in. List the first five things you would do.

1. _____
2. _____
3. _____
4. _____
5. _____

If you are greeting people as the receptionist, you don't have to stand and shake hands when a visitor comes into your area. You *do* have to stop what you're doing, look up, smile, and listen to what the person has to say. (Except for making eye contact, you should give the same attention to telephone callers.) If you keep typing or shuffling papers when visitors approach, they will feel that you're not interested in them or their needs. Never allow visitors to see your private moods or preoccupations.

Don't consider visitors to be an interruption of your work—no matter how much you have to type, no matter how often the phone rings. You should never be too busy to give a visitor a few minutes (but not the whole day!) of your undivided attention.

WHEN YOU'RE THE RECEPTIONIST (continued)

If someone else in the company needs to come out to greet the guest, call that person immediately and make a brief report to the guest: "Ms. Parkins will be here right away." If Ms. Parkins *doesn't* come right away, call her back and remind her, and tell the guest that you've spoken to her again and she *is* coming.

If *you* need to escort the guests to another area, always take the lead—whether your guests are men and you're a woman, or whether you're young and they're elderly, or any combination of the above. It's *your* office; you're the host. Lead the way, open and hold doors for them, and serve them first if refreshments are being offered.

On their first few visits guests should always be escorted to their destination within the office. Guests should also be escorted back to the main exit at the conclusion of the first few visits—or after every visit if your office layout is confusing.

Unexpected Guests

What about those guests who don't have appointments—salespeople, for instance? Managers rarely have time for all the people who want to see them. They often don't even have time for the people *they* want to see. If you, your manager, or your company has a policy about not seeing uninvited guests, tactfully explain the situation to the visitors, ask for a business card, and thank them for stopping by. Be pleasant. Tell them you'll put their card in your supplier file and that, if the need arises, you'll call them. This tells salespeople that you prefer to call them next time. Your politeness keeps your company from getting a reputation as being rude and hard to deal with. If the person calls again (in person or on the phone), explain that their card remains in the file and suggest they might want to write to the manager for an appointment.

While They Are Waiting

Sometimes visitors have to wait in your area until their host can see them. That can be uncomfortable for both of you if space is tight. There are a number of ways to make your guests feel more at home:

1. *Always offer refreshments.* If someone came to visit your home, you'd certainly ask, "Can I get you something to drink?" Your office visitors deserve the same courtesy.

   Many receptionists tell me they aren't allowed to leave the desk, or that it's too much trouble every time someone comes in, or that it's not *their* responsibility.

   If you can't leave, get someone to help you or direct the guests to the kitchen. Or put a coffeepot right out there in the lobby! If you don't have a kitchen (or lobby), direct them to the cafeteria. If you don't have a cafeteria, direct them to the water fountain. But you must mention coffee (or something) to everyone: "Ms. Gonzalez, I'm sorry I can't offer you anything to drink right now. If you'd like some water, there's a fountain just out to the left and I *can* give you a cup!"

2. *Tell them indirectly where the toilets are located.* Many visitors are embarrassed to ask about the facilities. Be discreet: "If you'd like some water, there's a fountain near the elevator, just to the left of the restrooms."

3. *Be sure they have a chair, an ashtray if smoking is allowed, and current reading material.* Although I know your annual report is fascinating, most guests might also like to read today's newspaper or the current *Business Week*.

WHILE THEY ARE WAITING (Continued)

4. *Show visitors where to hang their coats or offer to hang their coats up yourself.* Be sure your guests know where you've taken their coats. It's not necessary to help them take their coats.

5. *Offer as much assistance as you can*—such as looking up telephone numbers.

6. *Maintain a businesslike atmosphere.* When a visitor is near your desk, don't chat with friends or carry on personal telephone conversations. And don't smoke or eat or read with visitors in your area—even if they do.

7. *Engage in an extended conversation with visitors only if they begin it.* Since they may be reviewing their thoughts before seeing someone, chatting could distract them. If they start a conversation, reply in a friendly, businesslike manner. Be careful not to offer personal information about yourself, your manager, or your company's affairs. Try to stick to the weather, sports events, holidays, or other general topics. If they bring up a controversial theme, it's a good idea to shift the subject. No matter how strong your feelings, don't get involved in a debate.

What if they want to talk and you're very busy? It's not your responsibility to entertain guests (depending on the identity of the guest, of course). You've made them as comfortable as possible, and you have work to do. One factor that enters into this situation is the arrangement of your office. Is the guest chair next to your desk? If the guest seats are across the room, it's difficult for the visitor to carry on a conversation with you.

If you can't do anything about the furniture, be assertive. Answer their questions as simply as possible, smile, and turn immediately back to your task.

WHEN YOU'RE IN AN INSIDE OFFICE

You may need to go out to the lobby to greet guests who have come to see you or your manager. You may skip this courtesy for visitors who come often, but it's a good idea to go to the reception desk to meet all VIPs and first-time visitors.

Make a professional entrance into the reception area. When you think of making an entrance, it may conjure up visions of Scarlett O'Hara coming down the staircase at Tara. Your entrance should not be as dramatic or as grand as Scarlett's, but it's equally important. Every time you enter a room, someone is watching and evaluating you. Remember that you're judged first by your appearance, posture, demeanor, and other nonverbals—and the visitors' opinion of you may determine their opinion of the entire company. If you appear embarrassed, disheveled, nervous, apologetic, or timid, you lose credibility before you even open your mouth.

Make sure your posture, facial expression, and body movements are confident and reveal only what will be helpful to you professionally. Don't wear your feelings on your sleeve or allow the stress or disappointment of the day to follow you through the door. If you're negative when you greet people, they will probably reciprocate.

Receiving Guests For Your Manager

Introduce yourself right away: "Good morning, Mr. Widmeyer; I'm Brenda Bones." If you're the host's secretary, add that bit of information: "Good morning, Mr. Widmeyer; I'm Brenda Bones, Ms. Lyndall's secretary." If Mr. Widmeyer doesn't hand you a business card—and it's likely he would have one—don't hesitate to ask for it. It will come in handy later, for introductions and for your files. Give the card to your manager as you introduce the visitor, or simply put it on the manager's desk where he or she can see it.

When you show the guest the way to your manager's office, say something like, "Ms. Lyndall is expecting you. Please come with me." Avoid such abrupt commands as "Follow me," or "Walk this way."

If you look up and see a person who looks lost, it is certainly good manners to offer to help. But try not to sound suspicious or condescending because they're in your area when they should be in another area. People doing business in your office should not have to be cross-examined. If you suspect that person shouldn't be there at all, call the receptionist and check. If you don't have a receptionist, ask the person politely, "May I help you?" If he or she appears *really* suspicious, call security.

RECEIVING GUESTS FOR YOUR MANAGER (Continued)

If visitors stop by your desk or poke their heads into your office and ask how to find someone, be polite enough to help. People should not have to wander through your company's or your building's maze. Please don't just say, ''I don't know,'' and leave them to wander on. If they're in the wrong department, lead them or carefully direct them to the right department. If they're at the wrong company, check your building directory for them, or at least offer them a phone to call their contact and get directions.

When You're The Person Guests Came To See

If you, the host, realize you have to keep your guests waiting longer than ten minutes (which may be poor planning on your part), go out yourself and explain. It irritates people to be kept waiting and have no contact with the person they've come to see. If you need a while longer, give your visitors the option of waiting or returning at another time. If you and your staff are gracious and sincerely apologetic, your visitors' feathers won't be so ruffled when they *do* see you.

GREET YOUR GUESTS WITH ENTHUSIASM

SHAKING HANDS

The professional way to greet someone who comes into your work area is to stand, come out from behind your desk, smile with warmth and interest, and extend your right hand for a firm handshake. If you remain seated while someone is introduced to you, you convey a lack of interest—implying that you'd prefer not to be bothered. (Of course you don't have to rise every time a coworker enters your office, even if your visitor is a woman or someone of slightly higher rank.)

After shaking hands, greet the person verbally by repeating his or her name and stating yours immediately if someone hasn't already introduced you: ''Good to meet you, John. I'm Kay duPont.'' Or, ''It's a pleasure meeting you, Mrs. Smith.'' A greeting like, ''Mary has told me so much about you'' is not proper unless you have a valid reason for saying it—for example, if your guest has just married your close friend and you naturally *have* been hearing about him.

Shaking hands is the most established form of etiquette in American business today. It began as a sign of peace—proving that you weren't carrying a concealed weapon—and it remains a peaceable gesture. More than that, most people consider it an insult if you refuse to shake hands, regardless of your culture.

If you can't shake with your right hand for some reason, offer your other hand. If your disability is permanent, you needn't apologize for it. If it's temporary, you need only smile and say something like, ''My right hand's a little under the weather right now.'' You don't have to explain your entire accident. If someone asks, make your explanation short and simple.

Your handshake says a lot about you. A firm handshake (without pumping or clutching) shows confidence, warmth, openness, and sincerity; a weak, limp handshake indicates just the opposite. A bone-crusher handshake tells people you're a dominating, insensitive type.

''Pump'' the person's hand once or twice (about as long as it takes to say both names), but don't continue to hold on. Even if your introduction continues, let go of their hand. Lean forward slightly during the handshake, smile, and make direct eye contact. A handshake without direct eye contact suggests hesitancy, untruthfulness, or a feeling of inferiority.

SHAKING HANDS (Continued)

FIGURE 1   Three Handshake Positions

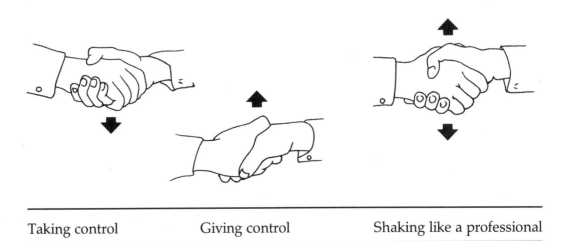

| Taking control | Giving control | Shaking like a professional |

When you shake hands, keep your hand straight, thumb knuckle facing upward. When people turn their hand so their palm faces down in the handshake, it transmits an unconscious feeling of dominance. You appear submissive if you allow the other person's hand to take the dominant position. This is a good handshake to use when you want to give the other person control or allow them to believe they are dominant.

In business situations, never double-clasp (put your left hand over their right hand), put your arm around someone's neck, put your hand on their shoulder, kiss (or air-kiss) their cheeks, or touch them in any other way. Be respectful of *their* personality style; not everyone feels comfortable with touching. Hugging and kissing are definite no-nos in the office setting, no matter how friendly your group or how close you feel to someone.

There was a time, not too long ago, when the rules of etiquette dictated that a man should wait for a woman to offer her hand first. No longer. Equality governs today: both parties extend their hands at the same time. Even rivals are expected to forgo their competition long enough to perform this small courtesy.

What do you do if you extend your hand and the other person doesn't take it? Simply withdraw your hand discreetly, don't comment, and don't feel any shame or embarrassment.

INTRODUCING PEOPLE

Although we may not be as formal as we used to be, introductions are still very important.

When you introduce someone, start with, ''Ms. Long, meet Mr. Roscoe from Company/Dept/State.'' ''Mrs. Brown, I'd like to introduce my son, Cliff. Cliff, this is Mrs. Brown.'' Never phrase an introduction as a command: ''Mr. Roscoe, shake hands with/meet Ms. Long.''

Next say something about the person being introduced. ''Ms. Long works in our Lingerie Division.'' ''Sally's a former neighbor of ours in Harrisburg.'' Providing this little bit of information to the group about the newcomer provides a topic of discussion so that the conversation can flow smoothly.

Refrain, however, from long stories about how you met, or about the person's life or background. Avoid phrases of superiority like ''Jeff works for me,'' or ''Sally is my girl Friday.''

PROPER INTRODUCTIONS

When Introducing	Name to Say First
Younger person to older person (Use youngster's first name, oldster's last—about 15 years is the deciding point.)	Older person's (Ms. duPont, this is Johnny Alexander.)
Peer in your firm to outsider	Outsider's
Nonofficial to official	Official's
Junior executive to senior executive	Senior's
Company executive to customer or client	Client's

INTRODUCING PEOPLE (continued)

Always present the older person, guest of honor, or dignitary first. Be sure to use titles, not first names, when introducing a much older person, a doctor (physician, psychologist, veterinarian, or PhD), a member of the clergy, or someone of official rank.

Use the dignitary's title even if that person is retired or no longer holds that position: "Governor Brown," "Mayor Taylor," "Colonel Johnson," "Ambassador Hadham."

When introducing a widow, give both her given and her late husband's names: "Mrs. (or Ms.) Greentree, I'd like to introduce my cousin, David Blackwood. David, this is Nancy Greentree. Her late husband, Harry, was a great friend of mine, and Mrs. Greentree founded the Elliot Institute."

An obvious breach of etiquette is calling someone by a name *you* prefer, not the name *they* prefer. An unflattering or juvenile nickname has no place in business. If Charles prefers to be called "Charles," that's what you should call him and how you should introduce him—not as "Charlie" or "Chuck." If you don't call him by the right name or if you mispronounce his name, it's acceptable for Charles to correct you in front of the guest. If Charles *prefers* to be called "Chuckie," that's his business. Don't assume you know what people prefer. I use M. Kay duPont as my professional name and I always present myself as "Kay." I'm continually amazed at the number of people who assume that my first initial, "M.," stands for "Mary" and bypass "Kay" altogether. They call me "Mary" or "Mary Kay," sometimes even after I've corrected them.

People are very sensitive about their names. Using incorrect names hurts your credibility and your chance of doing business with those people you've misnamed.

Being Introduced

When introducing yourself, or when being introduced, always stand and extend your right hand. If the person is older or a higher-level executive, say, "I'm happy to meet you, Mr./Ms. Name," or "How do you do, Mr./Mrs. Name." You may usually call younger people by their first names. If someone says, "How do you do," in response to your introduction, the proper response is, "How do *you* do," or "Pleased to meet you." "How do you do" is a greeting, not a question, and "Fine" is not the proper answer.

Remembering Names

According to Dale Carnegie, a terrific way to win friends and influence people is to remember names. Remembering—and using—names will help you stand out as a true business professional. But you may have to work at it; remembering takes concentration and desire. Some simple guidelines:

1. *Be sure you actually* **hear** *the name.* If people say their names casually, indistinctly, or too quietly for you to catch, ask them to repeat it. Rather than offending them, most people will consider it a compliment. Repeat the name slowly and distinctly so that the other person can correct you if you have misunderstood. If the name is difficult, spell it phonetically in your mind. If possible, write it down. If writing isn't convenient, *imagine* yourself writing it.

2. *Use the name as quickly as possible.* Using a person's name is a form of touch and a powerful means of communication. Don't overdo it, though; too much of a good thing can be annoying or sound condescending.

3. *Make note of the person's prominent features.* All people have certain features you can associate with them: the shape of their face or head, their hairstyle or complexion. Try to associate the features with the name.

4. *Find out more.* Ask about the person's job, hobbies, or favorite sports. Repeat the ideas to yourself. Make a link between their name and the facts again. Try to be interested *in* them instead of worrying about being interesting *to* them.

5. *Concentrate.* Look into the person's eyes, watch their lips, be aware of their gestures and facial expressions. In other words, shut out all distractions.

When You Forget A Name

The best thing to do when you've been introduced to people and you need to introduce them to someone else but you've forgotten their names is to be honest. Everyone occasionally forgets names; it's only human. If you *do* forget a name, don't panic! Simply admit your momentary lapse and say something like, ''How could I possibly forget your name? I just heard it!'' Or, ''I'm sorry. Please tell me your name again.''

If you can't bring yourself to admit your memory lapse, you can always fill in by telling some humorous or interesting information about the person. Or laugh and say something like, ''My mind's a mess today. Why don't you introduce yourselves?'' Pretty soon everyone will be smiling and introducing themselves. As they do, listen again for the names you've forgotten. The pause works well too—''Deborah, this is...'' The other person will usually jump in for you.

When you meet someone who has forgotten *your* name, don't make them suffer. State your name at once. And if you want to greet someone who may not remember you, approach by saying something like, ''Hello, Kay. I'm Abbey Lane. We met at Dr. Howser's office several weeks ago.'' This assertive courtesy will take the pressure off the other person and establish an immediate rapport.

INTRODUCING PEOPLE (continued)

When Introductions Are Forgotten

Far more rude than forgetting a name is not introducing people at all. People are usually very uncomfortable when they're not introduced as part of the group.

When you're expecting several people and they are arriving separately, introduce each person as he or she arrives. Just politely interrupt the group's conversation and introduce the newcomer: "I'd like you all to meet Ann Bradley, with duPont and Disend. Ann, these are our associates from the southeastern office: Susan Starr, Loren Morales, and Fred Farthing."

It's also impolite not to introduce everyone within earshot to everyone else within range as you escort someone through your offices. Some people are notorious for introducing the visitor to everyone except, say, the secretaries. It's as if the excluded people are invisible. Can you imagine how it makes the staff feel when they're in the group but are passed by?

If you're the one who's not introduced, take the initiative. Don't call attention to the slight, and don't *ask* for an introduction. Just stand, extend your hand, smile, and say, "Hi. I'm Clyde Katte, Ms. Dodge's secretary."

If you *are* introduced but others are not, you may certainly take the initiative to introduce them if they are standing next to you.

If you're seated next to a person you don't know in a meeting or at a business or social gathering, it's perfectly acceptable to start the conversation by introducing yourself.

Saying Goodbye

When escorting your guests back to the main exit, thank them for coming, shake their hands firmly, and make good eye contact. Make sure your nonverbals assure them that you heard what they had to say and that your manner conveys your appreciation of their visit.

> Just remember that the main rule of good manners in greeting people and making introductions is consideration for everyone. Even if you don't know the precise etiquette, if you put people at ease and show proper respect, your actions will be acceptable.

EXERCISE

Choose the most appropriate answer:

1. You're a salesperson being introduced to a potential client. Unfortunately, you've just been holding a cold drink and your hands are like ice. You:

   (A) Smile and greet the person, but keep your hand at your side for fear he or she will think *you're* cold
   (B) Shake, but apologize for your hands, explaining that you've been holding a cold drink
   (C) Ask the person if he or she will hold your hands until they warm up
   (D) Blow into your palms before extending your hand

2. Someone has just walked up to you and introduced herself, but you weren't listening very well and didn't get her name. You:

   (A) Don't ask again because you don't want to look stupid
   (B) Ask again because you don't want to alienate a potential associate
   (C) Go find somebody else so he can introduce himself to her and you can listen

3. You're the secretary for the senior manager in your department. When your manager introduces you to a new secretary, you:

   (A) Smile, remain seated, and wait for the new secretary to extend his or her hand in deference to your position
   (B) Stand up and offer your hand
   (C) Get up quickly and hug the new secretary to make him or her feel welcome
   (D) Explain that you're in charge here, and as long as he or she wants to play by your rules, you'll get along fine

4. A female manager comes into a male manager's office. He should:

   (A) Rise and greet her
   (B) Keep working
   (C) Look up and greet her
   (D) Stay seated, but enthusiastically say, ''Hey, Babe, what's happening?''

(continued next page)

EXERCISE (Continued)

5. You're the receptionist for a small company and have been instructed never to announce an unscheduled visitor without finding out why that person is calling. One day someone walks in without an appointment and asks to see the owner. The visitor gives his name, but won't tell you his reason for being there. You:

   (A) Ask for a business card and let the owner decide
   (B) Tell him you'll be glad to tell the owner that he is there, if you can tell the owner the nature of his business
   (C) Refuse to announce the visitor, telling him you're just following directions
   (D) Let him go right in

6. When introducing your supervisor to a client, you should first say:

   (A) The client's name
   (B) Your supervisor's name
   (C) Your name

Answer these from memory:

7. When being introduced to a woman client, is it proper for a man to initiate a handshake?

8. What are two good ways to help you remember someone's name?

9. What should you do when you forget someone's name?

10. What's the longest time you can keep someone waiting in an outer office without explanation?

Answers on page 113.

S E C T I O N

IV

Telephone Etiquette

ETIQUOTE
The bathtub was invented in 1850, the telephone in 1875. If you had lived in 1850, you could have sat in the bathtub for 25 years without having the phone ring.

—Jacob M. Braude

TELEPHONE ETIQUETTE

On March 10, 1876, Alexander Graham Bell made the world's first telephone call. Today more than 300 billion calls are made each year in the United States alone. In some cities, there are more phones than people. Most executives conduct at least 50 percent of their business on the phone and no matter what level you work at in a company you're likely to use the phone a great deal. It is vital that you know how to use the phone properly.

Think of all the settings in which you use a phone. You may be using a cellular phone while driving down the highway at 55 miles an hour, or talking to someone in another country or on another continent, or using a cordless phone while you're mowing the grass. In any situation, phone courtesy should be automatic.

The problem with telephones is that people can't be impressed by the size of your office, the smile on your face, or the clothes you're wearing. They have only two things to go on—your attitude and your voice. People who call your office only once will base 90 percent of what they think of your company on that one call. Believe it or not, callers can tell whether you're having a good day or a bad day, whether you've had enough sleep—even whether you're sitting up straight—while you talk.

As you read this, you're probably slouched in your chair and your feet may not even be on the floor. Right now, before you move, pretend that your office phone just rang and you're answering it. Say something like, ''Good morning, duPont and Disend.'' If you're *not* sitting up straight right now, try slouching just long enough to hear how that phrase comes out. Do you hear how dejected and forlorn you sound?

Now sit up very straight, stretch, take a deep breath, smile, and repeat: ''Good morning, duPont and Disend.'' Isn't it amazing how much lighter and more enthusiastic you sound? Your positive attitude comes across on the phone.

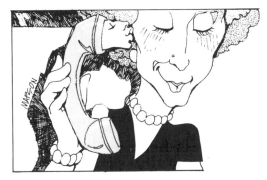

**IT ALL STARTS WITH THE SOUND
OF YOUR VOICE**

ANSWERING YOUR PHONE

Here are some principles for courteous phone answering. Check those you use.

☐ *Sit up straight, breathe deeply, and smile.* AT&T used to advertise as "the voice with a smile," but such voices are rare these days. Don't feel silly about smiling at a telephone—your voice sounds completely different when you're smiling. After you've reminded yourself to do it a few times, it will come naturally. And there's nothing more enjoyable than a conversation that produces a genuine, spontaneous smile.

☐ Unless you're driving or walking, *reach for the pad and pen* before reaching for the phone. This will enable you to take notes during the conversation to refer to or pass on to the appropriate party. Start writing as soon as the caller starts talking.

☐ *Answer by the third ring.* Answering promptly lets callers know you value their time, and that you don't expect them to wait while you're doing something else. Remember that callers have no way of knowing what you're doing—they only know you're not answering the phone. Quick service helps build a reputation of efficiency for you and your company.

☐ *Identify yourself immediately*—even on your car and cordless phones. In the office, give the name of your department and your name: "Book Department, Ms. duPont." "Book Department, Kay duPont." The first is more formal, the second more informal. Identifying yourself eliminates guesswork and saves time. It also promotes callers to identify themselves so you don't have to ask who they are. Even if they don't tell you their names, it becomes less formidable when you have to ask, because you've already introduced yourself.

☐ *Be courteous, friendly, professional, enthusiastic, and softspoken.* The principles for telephone etiquette are the same as for business etiquette: use good manners, project good voice quality, treat everyone with respect, and think about what you're saying. Talk into the telephone as you would talk to someone in your office.

☐ *Pay attention.* Callers shouldn't feel that they are competing with other things for your attention. Don't eat or drink or make remarks to people who pass by. If a visitor with an appointment arrives, try to end your conversation or put the caller on hold until you've taken care of the visitor. If you must divert your attention, explain to the caller and put them on hold. Don't put your hand over the mouthpiece—it's rude and people *can* hear you.

☐ *Transfer calls only when necessary,* explain your reasons, and ask permission first. Transferring is one of the most delicate areas of handling telephone calls. When callers are transferred from place to place, their good feelings about your company quickly dwindle. If you can help callers, do so. Don't tell callers that what they want isn't your job. When necessary, say something like, ''I'm sorry, Ms. duPont, I don't have that information. May I transfer you to the accounting department? I'll connect you with Brenda Alexander.'' Don't just say, ''Hang on,'' and let them go. Now and then, callers will not want to wait because they're too busy to hold. When that happens, say, ''Fine. I'll be happy to ask Brenda to call you back.''

☐ *When you must leave the line, explain why and return promptly with an answer:* ''Mrs. duPont, I can't locate that information. Give me a number where I can reach you, and I'll be happy to get the information and call you back.''

If you must leave the line to answer another line, apologize to the first caller and let him or her know you'll be right back: ''Will you excuse me a moment? I have another call I must answer.'' Tell the second caller immediately that you're on another line and you'll be back as quickly as you can. Even better, offer to call the second person back. The first caller always has priority over the second unless it is an important call you genuinely need to take.

When you return, regain the caller's attention by thanking them for holding.

> Don't leave people on hold for more than a few seconds. Letitia Baldrige says, ''There is only one thing worse in telephone manners than being put on hold, and that is being put on hold with music playing in the background.'' It's in effect saying that they will be on hold for a long time and the music is intended to soothe the savage beast. It doesn't.

☐ *React to the other person's conversation.* Even if you just say, ''Yes,'' ''I see,'' ''I agree,'' at least your caller knows that you're alive on the other end.

☐ *Eliminate as much background noise as possible.* Even though a radio may not bother you, it's magnified on the other end and can be extremely distracting to the caller.

☐ *End the call positively:* ''I enjoyed speaking with you, Ms. duPont.'' ''Thanks so much for your time, Kay. I look forward to meeting you.'' Then let callers hang up first so you can be sure they have completed their conversation.

WHEN CALLERS ARE DISCOURTEOUS

Sometimes you may have to handle callers who are not as well trained in phone courtesy as you are. Here are some suggestions for courteously handling these callers.

1. *When they talk to others while talking with you.* Suggest a meeting instead— when they aren't so busy. Or ask them to repeat what they said: ''Ms. duPont, it's difficult to hear you; it sounds like there are other conversations going on as well.''

2. *When they never seem to get to the point.* Use the direct approach: ''Kay, what exactly did you have in mind? How exactly may I help you?''

3. *When they don't even pause to breathe.* Interrupt: ''Excuse me, Ms. Neverstop, I don't think I'll be able to help you with this. It sounds like you need to speak with our accounting department. Please hold and I'll transfer you to Bennie Larson.'' (Yes, I know this breaks the earlier rule, but sometimes the situation becomes critical.)

4. *When they run on and on.* Take charge: ''Jim, let me quickly summarize what you've said and then if there's anything new or different, you can help me fill in.''

SCREENING CALLS

In today's hectic business world, it's a fact of life that most executives have their telephone calls answered by their staff. This often makes executives seem inaccessible and puts the staff members in an awkward position.

Because having their calls screened sometimes affects callers negatively, you need to be as tactful as possible. Demanding, "Who's calling?" *before* announcing that the person they want isn't in or isn't taking calls will only irritate the caller. If the person called will take calls but wants to know who's on the other end first, try something like, "Yes, she's in. May I tell her who's calling, please?" If she's only available to certain people, you could say, "She's away from her office for a few minutes. May I take your name and number and ask her to return your call?" It's just plain rude if the call isn't returned after he or she has been given this information; it tells callers they are considered unimportant.

If the person called is out, you don't need to explain their whereabouts. Say something like, "Ms. Volcheck is away from her desk. This is Brenda. I'll be happy to try to help you." Never tell a caller that someone is out of town unless you know the caller well. In the first place, it's none of their business; in the second place, you are compromising the home security of the person being called by informing a stranger that their house may be empty.

Never tell a caller *anything* personal: "I'm sorry, he's in the men's room." "I'm sorry, she just had a baby and had a few complications, so she'll be out for a while." "No, Mr. duPont just got a divorce and isn't feeling well today." Don't laugh—I've heard all of these!

Avoid the phrases, "He's not in yet," and "She's already gone for the day." It creates a negative perception for the caller. No matter what time of day it is, your coworker is simply "unavailable."

When you need to take a message, get the caller's name, phone number, company name, title if appropriate, action needed, and any additional data that will be helpful in identifying the person or the purpose of the call. A person who can take good messages makes an important contribution to any organization.

> Ask your manager to give you a list of people who should be put through without screening—family members, friends, senior management, Board members, outside consultants, attorneys. Ask each morning whether anyone special is expected to call today who needs to be put right through. Ask also for a good understanding of what constitutes an emergency situation and cause for interruption.

SCREENING CALLS (Continued)

Of course you'll get to know the voices of many regular callers. When you do, there's no need to ask who's calling or why. Just let the callee know who's on the line.

If you have instructions to find out each caller's business, you might say, "May I tell Ms. Hammond what you're calling about, please?" or "Ms. Hammond is not available at the moment, Mr. Rastow. If you'll tell me what you're calling about, I might be able to help you."

If you phrase your questions politely, most callers will answer them politely. Occasionally, however, you'll get an ill-mannered person who won't answer you. Just use common sense and remember that you're doing your job. If you've been instructed to get the callers' names, you have the right—and the duty—to insist that callers give you their names. Remind them that you're carrying out your employer's orders: "I'm sorry, but Ms. Hammond won't take calls unless she knows who's calling."

What if the caller gives you a name but refuses to tell you a reason for the call? They may say, "Kay knows what I want" or "What's it to you?" or even "Never mind who's calling. Just put her on." A good response would be, "I'm sorry, but Ms. Hammond won't take calls if I can't tell her the purpose of the call." Don't be frightened by high-pressure tactics, and don't become rude yourself. Remember that people who really have important business will tell you what they're calling about. Continue to make courteous requests for the information you need.

For more on this topic, order the Crisp Publications 50-minute book *Time Management and the Telephone* by Dru Scott, using the form in the back of this book.

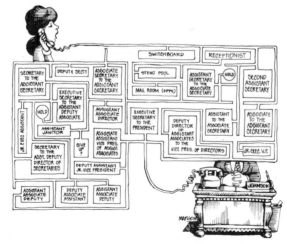

MAKING AND RETURNING CALLS

Whether making or returning a call for yourself or someone else, there are some basic points to remember and adhere to:

1. *Make your own calls.* I know it's prestigious to have someone else dial and hold for you, but it's also rude. If you're a junior executive calling a senior executive, you must be on the line when the senior executive answers, even if you've had your secretary place the call. If you call someone—anyone— outside your company, it's imperative that you be on the line when they answer.

   When you're very busy, it's acceptable to have your secretary make a call for you. She would say, "This is Ms. Rogers' secretary at duPont and Disend. Ms. Rogers would like to speak with Mr. Simpson. Is he in, please?" If Mr. Simpson is in, then Ms. Rogers should be on the line when he picks up. It's rude to make a call and say, "Hold for Ms. Rogers," and expect the person called to wait.

2. *Always return your phone calls.* If you don't, you're offending the person who called you...and all the people they tell as well. If suppliers call and you can't use their services, have the manners to call back and say no; don't make them continue to try to reach you indefinitely.

3. *Call only when you have a good reason.* A phone call intrudes into a busy person's day and should not be made without purpose.

4. *Call only during business hours.* Most people don't appreciate receiving business calls at home.

5. *Plan your calls carefully.* Know whom you want to talk with and don't call when that person is likely to be out or very busy. Remember to time your calls appropriately for time zones (most phone books have a time zone map). Make sure you dial the right number; if you do dial a wrong number, never hang up abruptly. Always make a sincere apology. (By the way, it's bad form to ask, "What number is this?" Ask instead, "Have I reached 234-5678?")

   If your call is answered by an answering machine, leave a complete message. I've had people leave messages on mine without a name. How am I supposed to know whose message it is? Leave your full name. As hard as it may be to believe, some people know more than one Kay or Jeff. Be sure to leave your phone number so that the person you called can call you back without taking the time to look up your number. Also leave the date and time of your call; it helps the caller to know whether this message came in before or after they last talked with you.

MAKING AND RETURNING CALLS
(Continued)

> If you own an answering machine that is used for business purposes, keep the answering message simple and professional. Owning an answering machine should not be considered an opportunity to enter show business. I think anyone who has ever been subjected to a comic routine or a tinny reproduction of someone else's musical taste will agree with me on this.

6. *Be courteous when your call is screened.* There will be times when you won't get right through to someone. Don't let this upset you; it happens to everyone. Explain your business to the staff member, and tell them if your message is urgent. Most secretaries and assistants are highly capable of relaying your message, and they can often be of great help to you. Being friendly and honest with the screener usually works in your favor. And it's bad manners not to leave a message of some kind. Don't say, "Never mind; I'll call back," and hang up. You also shouldn't ask the answerer, "Who's this?" If you really want to know, try a different tact: "This is Alex Bell. May I ask your name/who's speaking, please?"

7. *Greet the person you're calling politely, identify yourself immediately, and announce your purpose for calling.* Do this even when you call your best friends—they may have something else on their minds when the phone rings. Whether it's the first or the tenth time you've called someone, give your name. When you are using a mobile phone, identify yourself and explain that you're on a mobile phone; most of us realize that mobile phone calls cost by the minute, so your call may be handled quicker.

8. *Be brief; everyone values their office time.* If your call may take a long time, ask whether the caller has time to discuss the matter. If not, set up a specific time to get back with them. If you're calling someone's mobile phone, be extra brief. Discuss only pressing issues.

9. *Call back if you are disconnected from a call you placed.* It's your responsibility to call back.

10. *Hang up gently.* The last thing callers should hear is their name: "Goodbye, Ms. Donetti." Never slam the receiver in the other person's ear; it's comparable to slamming a door in the person's face.

11. *Use your fax machine if time is critical,* but understand that fax machines are not in our offices to excuse us from sending letters or making phone calls. They are designed for time-sensitive documents. If you need to get that message to several people, however, don't depend on the receiving party to make copies for you. Send a copy to each person who needs it. When using a fax, also remember that pencil marks and light blue ink do not transmit well. It's not mandatory to send the original copy of your message as a backup; faxed documents have been found by the courts to be legal and binding.

The telephone can help you win friends and customers for your company and build a reputation for efficiency and reliability. A solid reputation is important to your company's future—and to yours. Using the telephone to your advantage is really very simple: Just extend the same courtesies you like to receive when you're calling a business office.

EXERCISE

Test your telephone habits by checking the answer that best applies.

	Always	Usually	Seldom
1. I make my own calls and answer my own phone whenever possible.	☐	☐	☐
2. I keep a list of frequently called numbers to cut down on incorrect dialings and save myself time.	☐	☐	☐
3. When calling long distance, I dial direct and stay on the line while my call goes through.	☐	☐	☐
4. When taking or placing a call, I identify myself at the beginning of the conversation.	☐	☐	☐
5. I keep paper or telephone message forms and a pen or pencil by my phone...and I use them.	☐	☐	☐
6. I try to be informative and helpful when taking calls for others.	☐	☐	☐
7. When taking messages, I note the date, time, caller's correct name, caller's number (including area code), the message, and my name.	☐	☐	☐
8. When transferring a call or leaving my phone to get information for the caller, I tell the caller what I plan to do and then I place my phone on hold or put the handset down quietly.	☐	☐	☐
9. I give the caller progress reports on my efforts to find another person or the information requested.	☐	☐	☐
10. I offer to return the call if the caller will have to wait longer than one minute.	☐	☐	☐
11. I speak directly into the telephone, with good enunciation and an appropriate volume.	☐	☐	☐
12. I treat all calls as important and always thank the party for calling.	☐	☐	☐
13. Before leaving my phone, I tell someone where I'm going and when I plan to return.	☐	☐	☐
14. I immediately check for messages when I return to my desk...and I return calls promptly.	☐	☐	☐
15. I check the paper roll on the fax machine *before* I start sending my document.	☐	☐	☐

Answers on page 114.

S E C T I O N

V

Planning and Attending Business Meetings

PLANNING MEETINGS

Business people attend over ten billion meetings each year. The cost of these meetings is staggering. Even the cost of a small enterprise conducting a day-long meeting with ten staff members is high. In addition to the meeting room, coffee, meals, travel, and audiovisual equipment, you have to add the cost of staff members pulled away from their jobs. For this reason alone, meetings need to make good use of everyone's time. For a comprehensive book on planning, running, and evaluating business meetings, order the Crisp Publications 50-minute book, *Effective Meeting Skills*, by Marion E. Haynes using the form in the back of this book.

When planning a meeting, analyze your needs before you make any major decisions. Ask yourself (or your manager) what the exact purpose and overall theme of the function will be so you can plan to meet the right objectives. For some meetings, the primary objective is to get information to those in attendance (one-way, information *giving*). For other meetings, the objective is free-flowing communication, problem solving, participation, and discussion (two-way, information *sharing*).

Who Should Attend?

The purpose of the meeting determines who the participants will be. If the meeting is to provide information or ask for a vote on a previously discussed issue, the number of people attending usually presents no problem. If the meeting's objective is to study problems or examine issues and calls for analytical and synergistic decision making, the meeting may be more successful if you limit the number of attendees.

Once you determine how many will attend, it's wise to carefully consider who should be invited before issuing any invitations. When you have any doubt, meeting experts suggest excluding people rather than including them. You need to have the ''right'' people—those who *must* be there, not those who *should* or *could* be.

Give your in-town guests a minimum of 48 hours' notice, and at least two weeks for out-of-town guests. (Most people actually need more than this for a half-day, one-day, or two-day meeting.) If people are coming from out of town, include directions for driving or for getting from the airport to the meeting facility. Also tell them about nearby hotels, restaurants, pharmacies, and recreational and entertainment facilities.

PLANNING MEETINGS (Continued)

Even if the meeting location is familiar, people still need specific details like building number, floor, room or suite, and starting and ending times, on the invitation. Be sure to list a central telephone number to serve as a message center for participants and mention appropriate dress for the occasion.

Where Should It Be Held?

Real estate agents believe location is everything. In planning meetings, location is also a crucial decision, and the purpose should determine the place. Can you meet in your office? Which room? What is the most central off-site location? Do you want the atmosphere to be social or businesslike? Do you want a site with both business and social facilities? What should the meeting facility offer? What should be the layout for the meeting room?

Both on-site and off-site locations have advantages and disadvantages. Look at both to determine which will most appropriately serve your meeting's needs.

Consider the room size in conjunction with the number of people attending. A few people sitting in a large room can make the group feel uncomfortable. Too many people in a small room will produce a stuffy, claustrophobic feeling. How well the room is filled also affects the acoustics.

Conference Table Seating

The chairperson should always sit at the head of the table. You can easily indicate where the head of the table is: blackboards, easels, and screens should always be behind, or slightly to one side of, the head of the table, and the main door should face the chairperson. Figure 2 shows a variety of table arrangements.

Officers of the organization and other participants who will be addressing the group should sit to the right and left of the chairperson. If you plan a discussion format with no specific presentation, let the participants choose their own seats. If more than one person is attending from the same department, they may want to sit together so they can talk about issues as they arise (this could be disruptive in some cases).

ROOM SET UPS →

FIGURE 2 Conference Table Diagrams

ROOM SET UP	ADVANTAGES	DISADVANTAGES
Circle x x x x ( ) x x ( ) x x •Leader	a. Good morale for people b. Encourages open discussion	a. Hard to select a leadership position
Rectangle x x x x Leader• [ ] x x x x x x	a. Good for staff meetings b. Leader can assert control in front of room c. Encourages discussion	a. Limits number of people to size of table
Focused Rectangle x x x x x x [ ] •Leader x x x x x x	a. Creates leadership position b. Allows for more people than rectangle	a. Creates distance between leader and group
Doughnut x x x x [ ] •Leader x sits x x x anywhere	a. Equalizes status of group members b. Easy to see everyone	a. Limits number of people to size of doughnut

ATTENDING MEETINGS

Promptness

It's always bad manners to arrive late for a meeting—*any* meeting. In fact, you should plan to arrive a little early! If you are unavoidably detained, call and tell your host how soon you'll arrive. If this is impossible, apologize when you arrive and hope for the best.

> How long should you wait for someone when you have an appointment? Ten minutes is too long to keep someone waiting, but sometimes people do get involved in other business and forget they have visitors in the lobby. So, after about ten minutes, check with the receptionist or secretary. If you need to leave, write a message on your business card and leave it for the person: "Sorry. Had to get to another appointment. I'll call you this afternoon and see if we can reschedule."

Greetings

When the host or a representative comes out to greet you, or you reach the meeting room or host's office, extend your hand in a firm handshake. If there's a group in the room, try to shake hands first with the senior or most influential person in the group or the person you made the appointment with. Wait for your host to indicate a chair for you to sit on. Then sit comfortably, but erect and poised, with both feet on the floor, and don't fidget. Put your briefcase or purse on the floor. (See Section III for more on entrances and exits, shaking hands, and making introductions.)

It's not necessary to rise each time a peer enters. If the group starts to rise from their seats as you enter, you can simply acknowledge the courtesy with a smile, or say, "Please keep your seats."

When you are the meeting leader, start with a couple of minutes of small talk, then get down to business. When you are an attendee only, wait for the leader to begin the discussion.

Honoring Territory

According to many studies of nonverbal behavior, humans are territorial. Robert Ardrey, author of *The Territorial Imperative*, says we humans mark our spaces with our belongings, and we have a "comfort zone" we don't like others to invade without being invited. People who share a table or office unconsciously draw a line down the middle and stake out their side of the table. People who move into other people's space may be rebuffed for invading a private zone.

If you take up too much space in a meeting, you'll be considered rude. If you move chairs or other furniture to give yourself more space, those whose space you move into won't like it. It may also be considered an intrusion to look for something on someone else's desk, or to use their belongings without permission. It's one thing to handle someone else's pen or notebook when asked; it's quite another to take liberties on your own.

If you lean too far into someone's comfort zone, you'll probably be resented (particularly in male-female encounters). A safe distance in America is about three feet. More than five feet, however, may be considered too "distant."

To honor people's territory during a meeting (and also to look highly professional), pass out copies of your presentation so everyone can read it in his or her own territory. And don't put your copy—or any other papers, files, or personal belongings—on your host's desk or chair. Keep your things in your lap or on the floor beside you.

Touch

This form of space invasion must also be respected. The rule in business is: *Don't touch*, except for shaking hands. Other forms of touching are guaranteed to cause the wrong reaction, especially in a male-female situation. For more on touch, see Section III.

Keep Your Clothes On

Do not remove your suit jacket or loosen your tie unless the host or hostess does so or specifically makes the suggestion. If you do remove your jacket, don't put it on a chair; keep it with you.

ATTENDING MEETINGS (Continued)

Position Yourself

Sit with good posture, relaxed and comfortable, leaning toward the person you're doing business with. It also helps to know *where* to sit. In a meeting of only two people, you want to be to the other person's right side, not directly across the desk from them, with a moderate amount of space between you. Think about being someone's "right-hand man." When talking with two people or more, position yourself to see the reactions from all parties—at the end of the line or across from them all and slightly to the right side of the group leader. If you're a junior member of the group, however, you have to take your lead from the others. It's bad form for juniors to take their seats until the seniors are sitting or signaled to them where to sit. This rule applies whether you're in an executive's office, in the conference room, in a restaurant, or in a limousine. After you've been signaled to a seat, say, "Thank you," and go quickly.

If you're in a meeting with people you'd rather avoid, don't sit directly across from them—it's too symbolically confrontational. Choose a seat on the same side of the table, with one or two allies between you.

Use Your Voice Appropriately

Vocal tone, inflection, rate, and volume are a very important part of your business skills. What you say is often not as consequential as *how* you say it. Your voice should not be weak or overbearing; it should be calm and even. Avoid the roller-coaster effect of expansive highs and lows. Be aware of your breathing and don't let your voice sound breathy. Overall, be certain that your voice tone and volume are appropriate for the time and situation.

Listen

Listening to other people and being interested in them is one of the great keys of etiquette and diplomacy and the greatest compliment you can pay to another person. Some executives say they can actually tell whether people have been listening by the quality of the questions asked during a meeting. Your listening habits certainly become clear if you're required to make a summation of the speaker's main points at the meeting's end.

LISTENING (Continued)

Proper listening etiquette includes responding with appropriate facial expressions and body movements: leaning forward, moving closer, being attentive, showing interest. Use your eyes and lips to show that you're enjoying, commiserating with, or at least understanding what the other person is saying. Smile or frown, as the speaker does. Encourage people by asking appropriate questions. Don't finish someone's sentences, and always allow them to finish their idea before replying. If you don't understand something, ask questions to clarify.

When you don't agree, let the person finish, then try to summarize what you heard to make sure you've received an accurate message. Then state your viewpoint calmly and rationally.

Never interrupt. Interrupting stops the listening and evaluation process, and it's the worst kind of rudeness. For more on listening skills, order Crisp Publications' *The Business of Listening* by Diane Bone, using the form in the back of this book.

ATTENDING MEETINGS (Continued)

When Guests Arrive

In the business world, we still show deference to visitors, people in management, and our elders. We should begin doing this at an early point in our careers, and continue even when we merit such respect ourselves!

When a guest from outside the company comes into the meeting room or joins the table, the company people should rise and properly greet that person. When older, more senior members of management arrive, junior executives should rise and shake hands with them. This holds true whether the meeting takes place in a conference room, a restaurant, or the junior manager's office (unless the appearance is routine). Pay the same courtesy to senior executives that you pay to dignitaries, senior citizens, or guests from the outside. See Section III for the rules on greeting and introducing people.

Leaving the Meeting

If you are the one who called the meeting, you are responsible for ending it. Watch your host's time; don't take more than you asked for. When you have completed the meeting, stand, shake hands again, and leave with authority. If the meeting takes place in your office, walk your guests to the door.

If you were invited to the meeting, wait for the host or ranking manager to announce or indicate the meeting's end. Then pack up your belongings, thank people individually, shake hands, and leave gracefully. (If the meeting was with your manager or a higher executive, a handshake may be inappropriate unless you have just renegotiated your job responsibilities, talked about increasing your salary, or received a promotion.)

Remember to take any materials you received during the meeting as well as notepads, pens, or any other items you brought with you. Leave the room with your head and shoulders erect and confident, but also relaxed.

MEETING TRIVIA

Office meetings use 35–40% of the U.S. manager's working day.

Eleven thousand meetings are taking place in America right this minute.

THE JOB INTERVIEW

A job interview is just another type of business meeting. So whether you're the interviewer or the interviewee, and whether you're interviewing for a full-time position, a temporary position, or a contract position, the ideas and techniques we've already discussed in this chapter also apply.

Your résumé is the first impression the interviewer has of you; it needs to be top-notch. Don't send in something that's handwritten, or tattered and dirty and full of typos. It may cost you a little money to do it professionally, but it's well worth it. Employers look at a well done résumé and think, ''This person knows how to present herself and has a professional attitude. I want to meet her.''

Once you have an appointment, appearance and visual impact are especially critical. The quickest way to discredit yourself in a business setting is to arrive (or *conduct* an interview) inappropriately groomed or dressed. Studies show that most employers make up their mind about an applicant within the first thirty seconds. Even if you're hired, your relationship with the interviewer will be influenced by the first impression for a long time. First impressions have more impact than performance, family, or all the time you've spent to be well educated and knowledgeable in your profession.

You don't have to have a closet full of expensive clothing, but you do always need to look neat and conservative. If your clothes are too tight, your weight will be magnified and you'll look unprofessional. If your hair needs combing, your whole appearance will suffer. If your beard or moustache needs trimming, you'll appear sloppy. If you have body odor, no amount of talent or skill will get people to warm up to you.

It also improves your self-confidence when you look in the mirror and know you are tidy and well groomed. If you look like a million dollars to yourself, the chances are that you'll look like at least a thousand dollars to other people.

THE JOB INTERVIEW (Continued)

To decide what to wear on an interview, try to visit the company and see what the other employees are wearing. For corporate interviews or jobs in law or finance, dark, solid-color suits are the rule. In less conservative fields or smaller firms, many people are more comfortable wearing pants or skirts with a coordinating jacket. For creative jobs, the conservative "interview suit" may be inappropriate because creative people often have high visibility and have to look fashionable. But it's always better to be too professional than not professional enough. There are several excellent books on professional dress. Two are: *Successful Style* (for men) and *Always in Style* (for women). For more information, contact Crisp, Inc., at 95 First Street, Los Altos, California, 94022.

Nonverbal Interviewing Tips

Studies prove that 93% of your message is nonverbal—55% is in your appearance, 35% in your tone of voice, and 3% in your gestures. In an interview, try to use these nonverbal actions whenever appropriate:

- Maintain eye contact.

- Sit on the front of your chair and lean forward.

- Use your head and face to agree with both positive and negative statements.

- Speak at a moderate rate, volume, and pitch.

- Keep your hands in an open, unhidden position.

- Keep your legs, arms, and feet uncrossed.

- Keep still—don't fidget, drum your fingers, or crack your knuckles.

HOW TO BEHAVE DURING INTERVIEWS

1. *Be prepared to talk about yourself with confidence.* Be comfortable with the answer to the question ''Why should we hire you?'' When the interviewer says, ''Tell me about yourself,'' don't start fidgeting and fumbling and saying, ''Uhhhh.'' Interviewers often ask that question just to see how you carry on a conversation, whether you're sure of yourself, whether you're too confident or not confident enough.

Essentially, most employers want answers to these three questions: *Can* this applicant do the job? *Will* this applicant do the job? Does this applicant *fit* the job? Make sure you present your qualifications in these areas:

- *Ability, willingness.* Stress your outstanding accomplishments, skills, specific knowledge, intelligent ideas or concepts, and the personal attributes that separate you from other applicants. Be sure to include measurable information (for example, ''When I was product manager, sales increased 30% a year) and provide specific details. When mentioned early in the interview, these points make a memorable impact.

- *Flexibility.* The ability—and willingness—to learn new ways of doing things is a highly valued qualification. If you're new to the business world, stress your trainability. If you're an older worker or you're changing careers, you also need to be convincing about your ability to update and transfer skills to this new position.

- *Communication skills.* Next to job skills, communication is the most important attribute you can offer an employer. That includes, of course, getting along with other people. See Section II for more on communication skills.

- *Understanding the organization.* Put yourself on the company team. Don't go into an interview without having researched the company. Know what the company does and mention it often. Be able to say, ''Yes, I know about that project/acquisition/problem. I read the article about [your company] in _____ magazine.''

- *Good health.* Most interviewers want to know as much as possible about your mental and physical health. They are impressed by a person who looks fit and in control, and who seems relatively stress-free. They also look for a positive attitude and a sense of humor, because they know there's a strong correlation between those characteristics and health.

HOW TO BEHAVE DURING INTERVIEWS (Continued)

- *Honesty.* Organizations are always vulnerable to employee sabotage and dishonesty. Since interviewers are limited in the kinds of questions they can ask about your honesty, take every opportunity to express your commitment, integrity, and personal values. Allow your interviewer to feel that you won't cheat, lie, steal, or tell their competitors what they've been doing. Most employers believe, right or wrong, that the past is the best predictor of the future.

2. *Be prepared with answers.* You should already have thought about what questions the interviewer might ask you, and what your answers will be. Certainly you don't want to deliver a memorized response, but the more you practice your answers (try using a tape recorder to critique yourself), the less frightening the questions will be. Here are some common interview questions:

- Tell me about yourself.

- Why do you want to make a change?

- Where do you want to be in five years?

- What do you want from this position?

- What did you like most and least about your last position?

- How do you get along with other people?

- What was the most difficult situation you faced in your last position? What did you do?

- What are your three greatest strengths and weaknesses?

- Is there anything else you'd like to tell me?

3. *Use discretion.* Tell interviewers about your strengths. If they come right out and say, "What is your greatest weakness?" tell them, but describe it in a way that shows you are managing it well, and don't be ashamed of it. They want you to be honest, but they don't want you to put yourself down. They also want to be sure you can talk about yourself without stammering.

4. *Be prepared with questions.* When the interviewer says, ''Do you have any questions for me?'' have some. Show that you've done your homework and that you're interested. Your questions are a good way to reveal that you researched the company's products, services, and competitors. But don't ask, ''How much do you pay?'' or ''How much vacation do I get?'' (not in the *first* interview anyway). Don't lead the interviewer to believe that all you care about is the money you'll make. Ask questions about the company, the industry, and the particular job: What are the major priorities you see in this position? What do you expect me to accomplish in the first year?

5. *Use silence wisely.* Silence is powerful in an interview, and most interviewers are good at it. (If you're the interviewer and you haven't yet mastered this skill, practice with friends and coworkers.) In every interview, there's a time to talk and a comparable amount of time to listen. If you can learn to use silence to your benefit, and not just because you're too afraid to speak up, you'll have a definite advantage.

When the interviewer asks you a question, answer it to the best of your ability (briefly—don't recount your entire life history!) and stop talking. If the question is too general or doesn't give you a chance to adequately express your qualifications, you can always add the appropriate information. But if you talk too much or too quickly, you may lose your edge. Unless you're asked to give more detail, speak less than five minutes in response to each question.

6. *Be especially careful about touch.* When you're in an interview, you can physically touch the people you meet in only one way—by shaking hands. You can, however, use nonphysical forms of touch. For example, eye contact is critical. You must meet your interviewer's eyes before, during, and after the interview. When the interviewer says, ''Tell me about yourself,'' pull your chin up, make direct eye contact, smile, and tell them the information you've prepared. Don't stare, but don't focus too long on the floor or your lap when thinking or talking. If you have to look for the answers somewhere, look for them in the interviewer's face.

Another form of touch you can safely use is calling the interviewers by name. Repeat the name when you meet them for the first time. Call them by name several times during the interview (but not excessively). Use the name they have led you to call them; until they tell you differently, call them ''Mr.'' or ''Ms.'' Use his or her name again when you leave: ''Mr. Simmons, it was nice to meet you.''

The same principles apply if you are the interviewer. Don't lead the applicant to believe he or she is only a number or a warm body to you.

HOW TO BEHAVE DURING INTERVIEWS (Continued)

7. *Smile.* Not constantly, of course. If you never *stop* smiling, you might look like a kewpie doll! But, yes, it's important to smile. Don't even be afraid to laugh—appropriately and with dignity. Don't treat the interview process like punishment (no matter *which* side of the desk you're on); have fun with it! It's a challenge. If you look as though you're enjoying the interview, the interviewer will have a subconscious perception that you'll enjoy the job. And, remember, the interviewer may be just as uncomfortable as you are.

8. *Whatever you do, don't smoke!* According to a recent Robert Half International study, nonsmokers are much more likely to get and hold the top jobs in companies. The smoking rate of people at the executive level is 71 percent lower than staff personnel, and 36 percent lower than middle managers. A previous Half survey found that, when asked to choose between two equally qualified job candidates at any level—a nonsmoker and a smoker—decision makers chose the nonsmoker 15–1. According to Half, smoking darkens your career prospects. And nonsmokers can smell your smoke, no matter how long before the interview you smoked.

9. *Always send a thank-you note,* unless you're hired on the spot. See Section VIII for more on written etiquette.

For more information on interviewing, order Crisp Publications' 50-minute book, *Preparing For Your Interview,* by Diane Berk, using the form in the back of this book.

EXERCISE

Answer *true* or *false*. For those you answer false, what *is* the correct answer?

True   **False**

☐ ☐   1. The first step in planning your meeting is to decide where to meet.

☐ ☐   2. It's never necessary for a man to stand when a woman enters his office.

☐ ☐   3. A married couple should always be seated next to each other at a business function.

☐ ☐   4. Twelve hours' notice is enough for a company sales meeting with out-of-town reps.

☐ ☐   5. The head of the table always faces the door if possible.

☐ ☐   6. You should never burden the receptionist in your host's office about little things like hanging up your coat, directing you to the restroom, and so on.

☐ ☐   7. When you enter someone's office for a meeting, you should always choose the chair closest to the door.

☐ ☐   8. If you need to spread out your paperwork, do so on the corner of your host's desk.

☐ ☐   9. When you're not sure what type of clothing to wear to an interview, always choose a high-fashion style.

☐ ☐   10. When you feel the urge to smoke in the interviewer's office, always ask permission first.

☐ ☐   11. You should never ask questions during a job interview.

Answers on page 114

S E C T I O N

VI

Planning and Attending Meal Meetings

ETIQUOTE
We may live without books—what is knowledge but grieving?
We may live without hope—what is hope but deceiving?
We may live without love—what is passion but pining?
But where is the person who can live without dining?

—George Meredith

PLANNING MEAL MEETINGS

The business world has grown so complex executives expand their visibility by becoming involved with community groups and charities—and their lunches and banquets. Food and business cannot be separated anymore!

When a meal meeting is your responsibility, your involvement depends on the number of guests, the elaborateness of the meal, and how much planning the restaurant, hotel, or club will help you do. Much of your job as meeting planner is common sense. You can simply use many of the principles you would apply for a large dinner party at home, expand them, and make them more appropriate for business.

If you choose to have your meeting at a restaurant or club, remember that the facility you select will be perceived as an extension of your office. If you're taking one person to lunch, take that person's tastes into consideration. If you're planning a larger meeting, choose a facility where the food is good and the service is reliable.

If you often take people to lunch or dinner, it's good practice to become a regular at one or two restaurants so that you and the staff understand and respect each other's needs. Another advantage is that most guests are impressed when the maitre d' calls you by name and leads the party to your favorite table.

Call your contact at least two weeks before a small function and make the reservation in your name and the name of your company. Let them know how many will be in the meeting. You might want to ask for a remote table or a private room. If you intend to pay with a credit card, make sure they will honor it. It's even better if you can arrange to be billed for the meal so you won't have to deal with it at the table. Verify your arrangements the day before your meeting.

PLANNING MEAL MEETINGS (Continued)

When you arrive at the facility (before the others, of course), recheck your reservations (and your menu if you've preordered), and give the maitre d' an impression of your credit card so there will be no confusion at the table over who is paying. Wait in the lobby to greet the others; if there is no lobby, go to the table, but keep a close watch for the others. How long should you wait for a luncheon partner? Call the person's office about 15 minutes after the assigned time. If the staff doesn't know why the person hasn't arrived, wait 15–20 minutes more. Then either order or leave.

Make sure there's a place for coats nearby so they are safe during the meeting and people can easily pick them up after the meeting. As host, you should pay the coat check fee, with an appropriate tip.

If someone arrives wearing an expensive coat, don't insist on checking it for them. If others are checking theirs, say something like, ''Would you prefer to keep your coat with you?'' Then you can help your guest remove the coat if that seems appropriate. One of you should then put the coat on the back of the owner's chair.

If you and your guests are being led into the dining room by the maitre d', your guests should precede you and follow the maitre d'. If you're seating yourselves, take the lead. Be sure to offer the ''power seat'' at the head of the table to your guest of honor. Seat yourself with your back to the door or main part of the room.

If you're a man meeting with a woman, it's still polite to hold her chair as she is being seated (if the maitre d' has not done so). You do not, however, have to rise each time she leaves or returns to the table.

Let the servers know you're the host. If possible, introduce yourself ahead of time; if you can't, let them know through your eye contact and assertiveness. When asked if you would like drinks or appetizers, you can repeat the question to your guests to establish your position. Or, just to establish position, take the lead and say, ''I'm going to have a glass of wine. What would you like?'' If the server asks for your order before your guests', say, ''Please take my guests' orders first.''

Head Table Seating

When there are several tables involved, you may want to set your room with a head table for dignitaries. If you're honoring too many people to fit at one head table, set up a second. Place this table in front of, and lower than, the main table. (The main table, of course, will have to be on a riser.) If a second head table can't be arranged, use honor tables, placed adjacent to, or just in front of, the head table. Placards or tent cards may be used to indicate seating.

Head table guests are usually seated in this way (if you're looking toward the audience): The presiding officer sits to the right of table center (or the lectern) if the number of guests is even; in the center if the number is odd. The person with the highest rank sits to the right of the presiding officer, next highest to the left. The others alternate right and left according to rank. Those guests at the head table who have no official rank (such as the invocator) sit at the ends.

The presiding officer should introduce the head table in descending order of rank.

The seating arrangements for a regular table replicate those for conference room seating (see below). If you can't easily identify the head of the table, put the dignitary farthest away from the kitchen, facing the main entrance if possible. Husbands and wives are not normally seated together at a formal dinner.

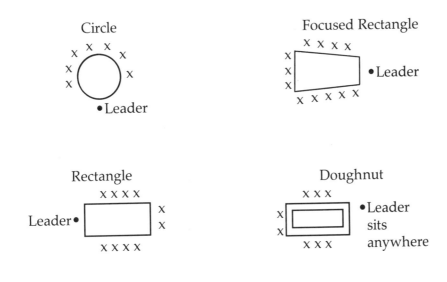

PLANNING MEAL MEETINGS (Continued)

Menu

When planning a menu, always consider various tastes and foods that may be unacceptable because of religious or other beliefs. Chicken is always safe, but certainly not the only choice. Most hotels and caterers are accustomed to meal meetings and offer other selections. You might also distribute a menu to participants beforehand with a notation that the facility can substitute entrees if you're notified by a certain time.

It's never a good idea to serve alcoholic beverages during lunch. It's also not a good idea to serve alcohol at a dinner meeting until the speakers have completed their presentations, although many businesses do. At large dinner meetings, entertainment is often provided after the keynote speaker, and this is a much more appropriate time to serve alcoholic beverages. It is best to check your company's usual practice and follow it.

Conversation

Relax for a few minutes before the meal with small talk, but avoid personal topics. Don't talk about your health or anyone else's. Don't ask questions about spouses or live-ins, especially to associates of the opposite sex. Avoid ethnic subjects (unless you're of the same background), religion, and politics. World news is appropriate; so is your business or another guest's business (never the business of someone not there). You may also ask about the well-being of common acquaintances.

Be careful with your compliments as well; personal comments may be perfectly acceptable to people you know, but they could be misconstrued by new acquaintances.

Remember that revealing confidential information, using insensitive humor, making sexist remarks, and berating your company or its staff are definite career killers. If alcohol affects your judgment in conversation, stick to mineral water at business events.

If you must interrupt a conversation, wait for a break in the intensity. Make eye contact and say, "Excuse me" when you must interrupt or leave the table or group.

If time permits, save your business discussion until after the meal. If that's not feasible, don't allow your business to be interrupted by servers; work out an agreement with the maitre d' ahead of time so that servers approach only at your signal.

> Never use dead-end questions like "How are you?" or "How's the weather?" or "Is is still snowing?" to begin a conversation. Questions that elicit one-word responses create awkward silences. If you want to invite conversation, try asking *who, what, where, when,* and *why* questions. Then listen. If you asked the questions, the least you can do is listen to the answers.

Paying the Bill

The check can be an embarrassing challenge, especially for a female host. The rule is quite simple: The one who did the inviting does the paying. The best way to handle this situation is to arrange the details with the maitre d' before the others arrive. Give him or her an imprint of your credit card and either sign it on the way out or have it automatically billed.

It's appropriate to motion to the server to bring your bill, or to ask for it when you're finishing the meal. If the server hasn't figured out who's in charge and puts the bill in the middle of the table, pick it up immediately without comment. Also avoid commenting about the total, although you may silently verify the figures if necessary to determine accuracy of the amount and the tip.

If you received the bill on a tray, look at it and replace it face down on the tray with your credit card or money underneath. If the bill came in a folder, put the card or money into the folder and leave it on the table. If the restaurant is extremely busy or if the server doesn't return for the folder within a couple of minutes, go ahead and put your payment on top of the folder. It's not as proper, but sometimes it's quicker!

Tipping

Confident tipping—without fuss or comment—can make you and your guests feel more comfortable. Tipping has become a customary part of business life, although it is still theoretically optional. It should be used to show your appreciation for the service you received, not given condescendingly to someone of lower rank, or just because you're supposed to. Don't reward lousy service, but, no matter how bad the food or service, never make a scene during your meeting. Bring any problems up later with the manager or write a polite letter outlining precisely why the food was unacceptable or the service poor. Always report unpleasant experiences; if you don't, management cannot correct the problem.

TIPPING TABLE–NEXT PAGE

PLANNING THE MEAL (Continued)

TIPPING (Continued)

The tip should be based on the amount before tax, and should not be added if a service charge has already been added to your bill. The usual tip is 15–20 percent for the server, 7 percent for the maitre d' (or half the amount of the server's tip if you prefer). As an ultimate tip, also inform the server's employer of excellent service.

Tipping should be done quietly. Hand cash to the maitre d' or wine steward, leave cash or the credit-card slip on the table for your server. Think about your tipping money ahead of time: carry small bills in a special pocket so you don't have to leaf through your wallet. See the following Tipping Table for guidelines.

Tipping Table

Here are some tipping guidelines for different kinds of restaurant service. Food and drink tips are based on the amount of your bill before tax.

Person	Modest Facility	Expensive Facility
Table captain (the one who supervises the servers assigned to your table and attends to any complicated service)	N/A	5%
Server	15%	15%–20%
Wine steward	N/A	$3–$5 per bottle or, in a very posh restaurant, 15% of the cost of the wine
Bartender	15%	15%–20%
Washroom attendant	N/A	50¢–$1 per person using the facility
Coatroom attendant	50¢–75¢ per coat	$1 per coat
Doorman	N/A	$1 for summoning your car or taxi
Garage attendant	50¢–$1	$1–$2

ATTENDING BUSINESS MEALS

The business meal—no longer limited to lunches—has become standard operating procedure in America. And you must be as sharp and professional at a meal function as you would be in the Boardroom, maybe even more so. In the Boardroom, at least, you don't have to worry about which spoon to use!

There's a story in the personnel field about a very successful business owner who always managed to hire top-notch, long-term managers. He once told an interviewer that, before he would hire a manager to work for his company, he would invite that person to lunch. If the person salted their food before tasting it, they lost the job. ''Lack of manners and stuck in a rut,'' the owner said.

Times haven't changed much. The social atmosphere of breaking bread together reveals a great deal about your ability to relate to others and whether you can be trusted with responsibility. A woman missed out on a good job because of lunch. She survived all the in-office interviews with the senior managers and, when the CEO invited her to lunch, she thought it was to close the deal. The host, however, ordered every unmanageable food on the menu for her—from an artichoke to a lobster tail. She couldn't handle the challenge and keep up the conversation at the same time, and she didn't get the job.

Breakfast Meetings

For time-conscious people, the breakfast meeting is perfect. But few meetings are as hard on attendees—especially those like me whose hearts don't really beat with conviction until after noon. To avoid this, prepare ahead of time. Do all your paperwork the night before and make sure you know the exact location of everything you'll need (including the car keys and the restaurant). Lay out your clothing and check for spots and wrinkles. Polish your shoes. Set the alarm for a little earlier; you may be moving slower than usual.

Listen to the news as you dress. Read the front page and the business section of the paper too. You can be sure that any morning person knows the latest information!

When you order your meal, think twice about messy foods like jelly doughnuts or soft-boiled eggs or bacon. They don't look good on your tie and don't sound good in your stomach.

ATTENTING BUSINESS MEALS (Continued)

The Three-Martini Lunch

Despite the government's attack on the three-martini business meeting, "doing lunch" is still popular.

Let's address that question right away: To drink or not to drink? Of course, drinking during an interview lunch is a definite no-no. Drinking at a business lunch will not polish your image either, but it's not the worst thing you could do. If someone else orders a drink and you want one, have one. *One.* Preferably wine or beer.

If someone at the table has had more than one (or ten) and isn't functioning professionally, the senior person at the table should bring the meeting to an end. (If your boss has had too much, that makes you the senior person.) Just stand up and say something like, "Well, what do you say to heading back? We have a lot of work to do this afternoon." (If the person came with you or works for your company, get them up and out. And, of course, don't let them drive.)

You (or the embarrassed person) can apologize to the guests later. If you're worried about losing your job, go back to work and explain to your managers what you've done. They will usually side with you. Don't bring the incident up again to the person who was inebriated.

Table Manners

Your napkin is the one on the left. Put it in your lap as soon as you're seated, or as soon as the host does if you're a guest. At a formal restaurant, the server will remove your napkin from the wine glass or serving plate and place it across your lap. If you need to leave the table, put your napkin on the table at the left of your plate and back onto your lap when you return. You may tuck the napkin into your belt (but not your collar!) if you think it will help you keep stains off your clothing.

When you're the host, you should order and be served last. Allow your guests to read the menu, and offer suggestions only if asked. When you're a guest, you may order whatever you wish, as long as it's not the most expensive item on the menu. Don't order seconds of anything—including drinks. It's rude to spend someone else's money without permission. (If this does occur, the host has every right to override the offender...usually with the excuse of time.) Remember that you may unobtrusively change or cancel an item after everyone else has ordered.

Your food will be served from the right—expect the server to reach over your shoulder. Lean slightly left as this occurs.

Like Mother taught you, keep your elbows off the table while eating, but you may rest your forearms there between courses. What you *don't* do between courses in America is smoke!

As you eat, use your silverware from the outside in (see Figure 4). The restaurant places it in that order for your convenience. Bring the food to your mouth, not your mouth to the food. When you finish with a utensil, use the resting position and finished positions shown below. A used piece of silverware should never be put on the table.

FIGURE 4   Using Utensils

Use utensils from the outside and work your way in.

The rest position tells the waitress that you're still eating.

The finished position tells the waitress that you're finished.

TABLE MANNERS (Continued)

Helpful Hints

- Scoop your soup *away* from you.
- Use your knife and fork to cut larger, flat pasta such as lasagne; use your knife and spoon to swirl long, string pasta such as linguini.
- If you have a shrimp cocktail, use your cocktail fork to hold your shrimp and take bites of it, rather than cutting.
- Use your knife to cut fruit from the core and your fork to bring the pieces to your mouth.
- When eating shellfish, hold the shell with your hand and eat the meat with a cocktail fork. Do not stack the shells.
- When eating steak, cut and eat one piece at a time.
- Use your knife and fork with lamb or pork chops.
- Cut or pull chicken off the bone with your knife and fork, then cut it into bite-sized pieces.
- Cut off the tail and head of a whole fish, cut along the backbone, fold the meat back, remove the whole skeleton and set it aside before you begin eating. You may ask the server to do this for you.
- Vegetables served in side dishes can be eaten out of the dish or placed on your plate.
- Never leave your spoon in the cup after using it. Put it on the saucer.
- To eat strawberries, hold them by the hull.
- Raw apple pieces may be eaten with your fingers.
- At a clam bar, it's acceptable to suck the clam off the shell. At a restaurant, use a fork for the clam, a spoon for the broth.
- You may spread cheese with either a fork or a knife.
- You may sip your coffee or tea with a spoon when it's too hot to drink normally.
- Eat limp bacon with a fork, crisp bacon with your fingers.
- You may eat the green ''fat'' from a lobster.
- Fruit pits go untouched from mouth to spoon to edge of plate.
- After using sugar out of a packet or butter off a paper square, put the paper under the edge of your plate, on the edge of your butter plate, or in the ashtray if nobody's smoking.
- Use a spoon to get jam from a jar, then put it on your butter plate. Use your knife to get it to your bread.
- Eat artichoke leaves with your fingers.
- You may eat firm asparagus with your fingers at an informal dinner.
- It's not necessary to cut olives or cherry tomatoes before eating.
- You may drink your soup if it's served in a cup with handles.
- Wineglasses are held by the bowl, not by the stem.

When you need to pass items around the table, always pass them to your guests first, usually counterclockwise. If you are asked to pass the bread or rolls, pass the butter too without being asked. When the butter comes to you, place a small amount on your bread plate. If you don't have a bread plate, put the butter on the edge of your dinner plate. Break your bread into small pieces and butter it one bite at a time, keeping the pieces on your bread plate or on the table next to your forks. If the server places coffee or tea on the table without pouring it, the person closest to the pot should offer to pour. You may reach for anything within easy reach, but not across the table. Never push your plate toward the center of the table when you've finished.

Excuse yourself for all biological functions, including the need to blow your nose. Blowing your nose on the restaurant's napkins—paper or otherwise—is very bad form. So is using a toothpick at the table.

Sometimes you may want to offer a toast for a job well done or a special event. If so, follow the KISSS rule: Keep It Short, Simple, and Sweet. ''Roasts'' are usually no fun for the person honored. If you're the person being toasted, you don't rise or drink the toast. You may do both when the toasters are finished. If you're a nondrinker, just raise an empty glass or a glass of soda.

ATTENDING BUSINESS MEALS (Continued)

Dinner Meetings

Tom Pettibone, a New York–based management consultant, said in a recent article, "Most of the deals in this country are locked up between seven AM and noon. The next most critical time is between five and nine PM. That's when a lot of businesspeople get together with possible clients—at dinner."

Dinner is slightly more formal than lunch—evenings demand a dressier look and ambience, but the rules of dinner etiquette are the same as those for breakfast and lunch.

One social skill that may be needed only at dinner is that of ordering wine. If you don't already have a passable knowledge of wines, it makes sense to learn. And there could be worse educational challenges than tasting a variety of wines!

If you're a guest ordering the wine, you may want to check with your host regarding cost. If it's appropriate and will not be embarrassing, ask if there's a ceiling on the wine budget. In lieu of that openness, suggest one in each price category and let your host make the final decision.

Although it really makes little difference if you drink red wine with fish or white wine with beef, you'll look more proper if you order them according to the honored guidelines:

- Red wine complements red meat, game, most pasta, and spicy food.
- Dry white wine complements fish and poultry; sweeter white goes with desserts (so does port).
- Champagne goes with everything, and it comes in a pony size (always a good choice for social drinkers).

Many people prefer not to drink red wine because it can go to the head faster than white, it sometimes causes an allergic reaction or headache, and it can be higher in calories. Ask your guests which they prefer; if they want white, order white. If some prefer red and some white, order half bottles or order a blush wine.

Thank-You Notes

Whether you were invited to breakfast, lunch, tea, dinner, or a reception, always send your host a handwritten thank-you note.

Can You Refuse?

Sure, as long as you're willing to face the consequences. Many people consider a business meal a waste of time, but the choice is yours. If your manager asks you, you probably should go. If suppliers ask, you have every right to tell them that your decision in no way affects your doing business together, but you prefer not to be entertained by vendors.

EXERCISE

Answer *true* or *false*. For those you answer false, what *is* the correct answer?

True   **False**

☐   ☐   1. You and your manager were supposed to go to a business luncheon together with several good clients. You've arrived, but your manager has not. When the clients start to order alcoholic drinks, you should order a drink, because it won't look good to be out of synch with your clients.

☐   ☐   2. Wineglasses should be held by the bowl, not the stem.

☐   ☐   3. It's never acceptable to sip your coffee or tea with a spoon.

☐   ☐   4. As host at a business dinner, you should place the highest-ranking guest on your left.

☐   ☐   5. When meeting a client for lunch, always wait for your guest in the bar or at your table.

☐   ☐   6. When a woman invites her male client to discuss business over lunch, the man should always pay.

☐   ☐   7. When a man and a woman are escorted to a dining table, the man immediately follows the maitre d'.

☐   ☐   8. You should always take the first roll from the basket and then pass to your guests.

☐   ☐   9. You should always tip your servers at least ten percent.

☐   ☐   10. You must cut the olives and cherry tomatoes in your salad before eating them.

Answers on page 115

S E C T I O N

VII

Business Invitations and Gifts

ETIQUOTE
"We must learn to balance the material wonders of technology with the spiritual demands of our human nature."

—John Naisbitt
Megatrends

SENDING INVITATIONS

The most important rule in sending invitations is understanding your guest. Take into consideration the kind of relationship you have with this person and what he or she likes to do, and extend your invitation accordingly.

Inviting Your Boss

It's not usually proper for a junior person to invite the boss to dinner—unless you have become social friends. If you've been entertained in your employer's home when other people were also invited, don't feel compelled to return the invitation. If you *do* want to entertain your boss and you're even the least bit hesitant about doing so, it may be better not to entertain at your home. Many people are uncomfortable with their employer in a private setting, and dinner at home is no time to try to *create* rapport. It's also hard to judge whether you've overdone or underdone your entertainment. Never invite your boss to your home strictly because you think it will help your career.

SENDING INVITATIONS (Continued)

Inviting Another Executive

What if two executive couples want to get together for an evening? Should the wife of one call the wife of another? What if the executive *is* the wife? Actually, if the spouses don't know each other, it might be more appropriate just to have lunch! But sometimes it's a nice career booster to invite another business associate for a social evening and, of course the spouse must always be invited, especially if the event occurs on a weekend. If you invite an associate who has no spouse and yours is going, include an invitation for a guest, but not a *specific* guest (Millie and Joe might be having an argument that weekend).

Today's etiquette allows peers—men and women—to invite each other to social functions. If the invitation will be extended by phone, it's often easier for nonworking spouses or spouses with less hectic schedules to call on behalf of the couple, but this is no longer a requirement of social etiquette. It seems much friendlier for the people who know each other to make and accept invitations (after checking with their spouses, of course).

> Even with today's looser etiquette rules, a male and female dining together at night in their hometown may cause embarrassment. Lunch is a better way to socialize in this case. Dining together out of town should not invite gossip...unless the evening extends into the morning.

Invitation Stationery

If you want to make sure your invitations are noticed, send them on high-quality personal stationery (7" × 9" or smaller), handwritten or formally engraved, in a matching envelope with an appropriate festive stamp. Never type invitations—even those for business functions—or their envelopes, and never use a postage meter to mail them.

For formal invitations, it is common practice to enclose an RSVP card. If you do, make it easy for the guests to fill in their name, or fill it in for them. Always enclose a matching envelope as well (no smaller than 3½" × 5" because of postal regulations).

The more notice you give your guests, the more likely they are to attend. Here are some guidelines:

- If the guests must come from out of town for your event, mail the invitations two to four months ahead of time.
- For a routine business lunch, extend the invitation at least three days (preferably a week) before.
- For a food or cocktail function, invite guests two to four weeks before the date.

RESPONDING TO INVITATIONS

Although you might make a greater effort to attend your manager's or an important client's social affair than you would for that of a co-worker or supplier, your decision should never be reflected in your response. Timing and correctness should always be the same.

The most important letters in the etiquette of invitations are RSVP. RSVP does *not* mean "Let us know if you're coming." It means, "Let us know *either way.*" Failure to reply to an invitation is a definite blunder (unless you've somehow contributed money for the invitation). Of course if the invitation specifies "Regrets only," you needn't acknowledge acceptance, but you *do* need to let the host know if you cannot make it.

Informal and oral invitations may be handled with less formality, but meeting your host in the hallway and saying, "Hey, thanks for the invitation. We'll be there!" does not constitute an RSVP. To respond to an informal invitation, either call the host or write a personal note.

When you are responding to a formal invitation, accept or decline in writing on personal stationery—unless you are using an RSVP card (see Section VIII). Include the wording used in the invitation and state clearly whether you will or will not be attending. You do not need to explain why you are declining in detail. Always use a stamp (preferably an attractive commemorative), never a meter imprint. Your response may be made either one to one or couple to couple. If your invitation includes a guest, give the full name of the person attending with you and their relationship to you.

Example of Acceptance

Mr. and Mrs. Herman LaCross accept with pleasure your kind invitation for dinner on Saturday, November 5, at 8:00 p.m.

Example of Regret

Mrs. Elaine Goodrich and Mr. Jack Ortiz regret that a previous engagement prevents their accepting your kind invitation for dinner on Saturday, November 5, at 8:00 p.m.

RESPONDING TO INVITATIONS (Continued)

Respond to any invitation—formal or informal—within 24 hours if possible (three days maximum). Your host is investing both money and time, and will appreciate being able to plan accurately. If you are uncertain whether you will be able to attend, let the host know immediately, and let him or her know when you will be able to respond, making sure that the date does not interfere with the event's arrangement.

Never cancel an acceptance for any reason other than an urgent one. If you absolutely must cancel, make the call or write the note yourself; don't ask someone else to do it for you. It's equally rude to send someone in your place if you have agreed to be there, and to bring uninvited guests.

If the person invited is away and will not be back in time to return the RSVP, his or her secretary (assistant, housekeeper, etc.) may phone the host or return the RSVP card. If the invitee knows the host well, the secretary should include a note with the RSVP, explaining the employer's absence: ''Ms. duPont is unable to respond herself because she is out of town on a business trip and won't return until after your dinner party. She asked me to thank you for your thoughtful invitation.''

Just as RSVP are magic letters, ''Thanks'' is a magic word. Thank-you notes don't need to be long, but they do need to be sent for *any* event hosted by another. Any lapse of time over 48 hours is unforgivable.

Of course there are always office events that don't require an RSVP because they are command performances—the summer picnic, the holiday party. Should you go? Probably. Should you drink? Probably not. Should you stay very long? No. Go and have a good time and be seen by everyone. Shake hands, raise your cola for the toasts, and dance with the boss or the boss's spouse if you want. But, for the sake of your future, wear your best party or play clothes, or your least revealing evening clothes; don't talk too loud or too much; and ignore the mistletoe.

GIVING BUSINESS GIFTS

Business gift-giving is considered appropriate by most companies and individuals, although some organizations forbid the practice. And there are some laws you may need to consider. The Federal antibribery law, for instance, forbids gift-giving by customers to officials of financial and government institutions. (Check with your local IRS office regarding regulations on gift-giving if you have any doubts.) As with all things, appropriateness and good taste are the keys. The type of gift, its value, the reason given, and how it is presented often determine its acceptability. Here are some considerations for business gift-giving:

1. *Timing.* Don't wait six months after your client's wedding to send a gift. Send clients your new product sample *before* it hits the stores. Send holiday presents 10–15 days prior to the holiday.

2. *Reason.* Birthday presents aren't necessary, but are perfectly proper. So are gifts to say thank you, to encourage someone, to express sympathy or health wishes, and to congratulate. It's not mandatory to give your boss a holiday gift, especially if you're a receptionist, secretary, or staff assistant. You may if you want to, but make it modest and impersonal (a book, a bottle of wine, a tree ornament, a box of cookies). If you're new to the company—even in an executive position—don't give your boss a present; it might be misconstrued.

3. *Culture.* Consider the recipient's culture. For example, it's insulting to take a clock (and many other things) to Japanese people. And if you do give them a gift, they may feel obligated to give you one in return. They're great gift-givers! So are the Arabs. If an Arab gives you a present, he or she expects an equally expensive or appropriate gift from you. (For more on intercultural etiquette, see Crisp Publications, *Working Together*.) Even Americans have different tastes: Those of the Jewish faith may not appreciate Christmas gifts; liquor is not an acceptable gift for teetotalers; ashtrays are not appropriate for nonsmokers.

4. *Personalization.* A business gift for an individual should always be something you know recipients will receive pleasure from, selected specifically for *that* person. Knowing their hobbies and interests can make gift selection easier. For practically every interest or hobby, you can find books, magazines, gadgets, and a host of other items within your price range. Most major department and specialty stores provide a free gift-buying service. These services look for the type of gift people might want but generally won't buy for themselves.

   It's best to stick with a more general gift if you have any doubt about the person's interest or hobbies. Although *personalized* gifts show thought and planning, *personal* gifts like clothing and intimate items show a lack of professionalism.

GIVING BUSINESS GIFTS (Continued)

If you're totally at a loss, you might consider a gift certificate from a quality department store, specialty store, or catalog that stocks a particular type of merchandise. Remember, though, that some people view gift certificates as impersonal and don't appreciate them. If you have any inkling that the recipient wouldn't appreciate such a gift, make another selection. When in doubt, always play it safe.

When your customer's company is sensitive about personal business gifts, it may still be appropriate to give food gifts that can be shared by the whole department: ten pounds of pistachios, or twenty pounds of chocolates, for example.

5. *Amount.* It's seldom proper to spend lavish sums on business gifts (including lunches or dinners). Ten to twenty-five dollars is an appropriate price range for your manager, except for a CEO or upper-level executive, in which case $25–$50 is acceptable. Client gifts should usually run $10–$25. Fifty to one hundred dollars is for the executive-to-executive level. Gifts of more than $100 are only for *very important* occasions and people. Know what's common in your organization and in your industry, and stay within your range. Just because your boss gives you a $50 gift doesn't mean you have to give him or her one of equal value.

If two or more people share a secretary, receptionist, assistant, or even a manager, they might want to chip in $5–$15 each and buy her or him something nice, presented with a card signed by everyone who contributed.

*MAKE SURE THE PRICE OF YOUR
GIFT IS APPROPRIATE.*

DON'T GO EMPTY HANDED

If you're invited to an event honoring someone—a wedding, christening, confirmation, bas or bar mitzvah, anniversary or graduation parties, and so on— a gift is definitely in order, even if you can't attend. The value of the gift should not be affected by your ability or inability to attend. If you don't receive a thank-you within ninety days, call and ask whether they received the gift. If the event is called off, you should expect to receive your gift back. If the event is for *you*, send flowers to the hostess before the party.

House gifts are customary when you attend a dinner party, open house or similar function—especially at holiday time. The gift doesn't have to be expensive—a bag of flavored coffee, a loaf of homemade bread—but it does need to be handed to the host or hostess on arrival. Don't urge your host or hostess to open it, however, unless it's something that concerns the entire party. If you want to share in their delight with the gift, leave it unwrapped. Put a festive bow on the gift or buy something in a decorative container.

You may personally deliver your gifts or send them by mail or courier, preferably to the recipient's home (especially liquor). Personal delivery always seems much warmer, but personally delivering a business gift to an individual's home is inappropriate unless you've been invited there for a specific occasion.

Always include a handwritten note with the gift, on notepaper or a greeting card (not your business card) in an envelope.

A gift is not required if you don't attend. You'll be thoughtful and proper, however, by sending flowers or a bottle of champagne to the house the day of, or the day before, the dinner party. Send a brief note with the gift, such as: "We hope you and your guests have a delightful evening." The note should not refer to your lack of attendance.

GIVING GIFTS (Continued)

Tasteful gifts to consider:

- A gold or silver pen
- Flowers or plants (yes, a woman may send flowers to a man!)
- An attractive appointment book or calendar
- An engraved key ring
- An elegant bookmark
- A basket of gourmet coffees, teas, cheeses, or fruit
- A bottle of champagne, or a favorite wine or liquor
- Pressurized balls for a tennis player
- Lures, tackle box, or other gear for a fishing enthusiast
- Special key holder or timepiece for a jogger
- Goggles, gloves, or hat for a skier
- Odometer or bike gloves for a cyclist

Gifts you should never give:

- Anything overly expensive
- Perfumed stationery
- Anything smutty, sarcastic, sexual, or extremely personal
- Animals
- Liquor to nondrinkers, candy to dieters, etc.
- Clothing (wallets and handbags are acceptable)
- Anything oversized or fragile to someone who has to fly with it
- Perfume or cologne unless you know their preferred fragrance
- Anything of inferior quality

RECEIVING BUSINESS GIFTS

You'll have to use judgment about whether to accept a gift. Unfortunately, you usually can't make that decision until you've opened it. If you think keeping the gift might show poor judgment, put it to the appearance test: A gift should never appear to be a bribe or represent a conflict of interest. It should be an acknowledgment from one business colleague to another, nothing more.

Ask yourself the following questions:

- Does the gift have excessive value?
- Was it presented at a nontraditional or noncustomary time?
- Does it violate company policy?
- Does it make you feel obligated to the other party?
- In the last three or so months, did you complete a business transaction that was of benefit to the giver?
- Is there a pending business transaction?
- Does the giver have a reputation of ''buying'' people?

If you answer *yes* to even one of these questions, it might be best to decline the gift. It's always better to err in favor of declining a gift than to accept a questionable one.

If you decide to decline the gift, do so within 24 hours. Lack of action constitutes acceptance. Return the gift with a handwritten note making it clear that you can't accept. You don't have to give a specific reason. Date the note and clearly state that you received the gift and must refuse. Be brief, but don't scold, insult, or convey a negative tone. If company procedures require that you report such actions, do so and keep a copy of the note for your own protection.

Sample note for refusal based on company policy:

Dear Joan: Thank you for the (gift) you thoughtfully sent me on (day and date). I sincerely appreciate your sentiments, but company policy forbids me to accept this gift. I'm returning it to you with this note/by Federal Express (courier, separate cover, etc.) today.

Sample note for refusal based on personal preference:

Dear Joan: Thank you for the (gift) you thoughtfully sent me on (day and date). I sincerely appreciate your sentiments, but the gift is not appropriate for me to keep. I'm returning it to you with this note/by Federal Express today.

RECEIVING BUSINESS GIFTS (Continued)

You do not need to telephone the gift-giver before returning the gift, nor should you bring up the incident in conversation later. If the giver mentions the return, simply repeat what you said in the note or tactfully move on to another topic.

If the giver contacts you to apologize, graciously accept the apology and don't mention it again.

When accepting a gift, acknowledge and express appreciation for it as soon as possible. Many people believe that a telephone call expresses enough thanks; perhaps, but it isn't good etiquette. A simple, warm, handwritten note such as the one below is much more proper, more effective, and more appreciated:

> Dear Mike,
>
> Thanks so much for your thoughtfullness in selecting the beautiful crystal cat for me. I don't have one at all like it in my collection! I'll think of your kindness and our association every time I look at it.
>
> Regards,
> Sally

Your note should always be on proper stationery or a thank-you card, not scribbled at the bottom of a business letter. If more than one person was involved, ask the recipient to convey your thanks. Mention them even if you don't know their names: "Please tell your staff how much I appreciate their part in this lovely gift."

Don't overdo it, though. One sincere thank-you in a note will suffice. And a thank-you note never demands a thank-you note in return! Remember Shakespeare's immortal words: "Me thinkest thou doest protest [thank] too much."

EXERCISE

Answer *true* or *false*. For those you answer false, what *is* the correct answer?

True	False	
☐	☐	1. You don't have to send a wedding present if you don't plan to attend the wedding.
☐	☐	2. A woman should never send flowers to a man unless he's hospitalized.
☐	☐	3. It's rude to return a gift.
☐	☐	4. You don't have to send thank-you notes to close friends.
☐	☐	5. The best gift for a Japanese client is a clock.
☐	☐	6. You don't have to thank people for a party at their house if you took a gift.
☐	☐	7. When your boss invites you for lunch or dinner, you must reciprocate.
☐	☐	8. RSVP means "regrets only."
☐	☐	9. Invitations to a formal dinner may be handwritten.
☐	☐	10. A gift certificate is the perfect answer in business gift giving.

Answers on page 115

S E C T I O N

VIII

Etiquette for Business Correspondence

ETIQUETTE FOR BUSINESS CORRESPONDENCE

In today's world, everyone writes, almost everyone types, and few know the rules of correspondence etiquette because the guidelines have changed so much. Without the proper correspondence etiquette for today's business, however, you may offend your readers before they even open your letter or finish reading your electronic mail.

There are three primary types of correspondence: official business, informal business, and personal. Figure 5 shows permissible forms for each.

FIGURE 5   Official Business

M. Kay duPont, CPS
Vice President

September 9, 19_____

Ms. Maryhad A. Littlelam
Fleece Animal Training School
Sheep Department
PO Box 123, Emu Station
Suretogo, GA 30067

Dear Ms. Littlelam:

The most preferred business letter style today is the Full Block. It is seldom used for personal letters. In this style, everything, including the date and complimentary close, begins at the extreme left. There is a double space between paragraphs and there are no indentions.

In America, this style always takes a colon after the salutation and a comma after the complimentary close.

Sincerely,

(Ms.) M. Kay duPont

aa

The three parts of a business letter most subject to errors in etiquette are the address block, the salutation, and the signature block. If you master the rules for these three parts of a letter and use proper spelling and grammar in your correspondence, your letters will have much more impact.

FIGURE 5: EXAMPLES OF BUSINESS LETTERS (Continued)

Informal Business

July 21, 19____

Dear Jack and Jill:

The Informal Business style is reserved for personal letters typed on monarch (7½″ × 10″) or half-sheet (5½″ × 8½″) stationery.

The structural parts differ from Full Block only in the position of the inside address. Place the salutation 2–5 spaces below the date line, flush left. The inside address is also flush with the left margin, but it goes 2–5 spaces *below* the final signature line.

Regards,

M. Kay duPont, CPS

Mr. and Mrs. Jack Beanstalk
135531 Empty Pail Road
Waterfall, Connecticut 06430

Personal (handwritten or typed on plain stationery)

July 21, 19__

Dear Jack and Jill,

A simple handwritten note is always appreciated.

Make sure your handwriting is legible and neat.

Regards,
Kay

THE INSIDE ADDRESS

Whether you're writing a formal or informal business letter, the inside address typically includes:

1. Addressee's courtesy title and full name
2. Business title or department
3. Full name of the business
4. Full address, including zip code

In a personal letter, of course, only items 1 and 4 are included.

The inside address begins 3 to 8 (but never more than 12) lines below the date. It's always single-spaced and blocked left. For a more professional look, avoid abbreviations in the inside address.

Courtesy Titles

Always use a courtesy title before the addressee's full name if you're sure of gender. If you don't know the person's gender and can't figure it out, use no title at all in the inside address and salutation.

None of us has any trouble with the courtesy title *Mr.*, but a problem sometimes arises when writing to a woman. Some women still sign their letters *Mrs. Jane Doe*, properly with the *Mrs.* in parentheses. If that's the case, you must address her as *Mrs.*, because that's what she prefers to be called. But when you don't know, as is more often the case, just use *Ms.*

Then there's the title *Dr.* A doctor is a doctor whether an *M.D.*, a *Ph.D.*, a *D.V.M.*, or an honorary doctor. But if you address her as *Dr. Jane R. Smith*, do not use academic degrees after her name. If you want to use her degrees, it's *Jane R. Smith, D.D.S.* This rule also applies to attorneys (*Nancy Bunker, Esq.* or *Billy Goforth, J.D.*). The only title that comes after the name and also takes a courtesy title is one designating inheritance—*Jr., Sr., II, III,* etc. (*Mr. John R. Smith, Jr.*). Incidentally, the comma and period are now optional (for *them*) with a title designating inheritance, and generation titles may be written in Roman numerals (*I, II*) or ordinals (*2nd, 3rd*). Follow your addressee's lead.

If your addressee happens to be plural, it becomes somewhat complicated.

RULES–NEXT PAGE

Business Etiquette and Professionalism

RULES REGARDING TITLES

Men:	Messeurs or Messrs. duPont, Disend, Bradley, and Alexander Messrs. Jim Smith and James Jones Mr. James Jones and Mr. Jim Smith
Women: **Married:**	Mesdames or Mmes., or separate names as above (with Mrs.)
Single:	Misses or Msses., or separate names as above (with Miss)
In general:	Mses., or separate names as above (with Ms.)
Male and female with different names (even if married):	Use two lines, with the man's name on the bottom line, or add *and* or a slash and use one line: Ms. Bertha Brown Mr. Wallace Wilder Ms. Bertha Brown and Mr. Wallace Wilder Ms. Bertha Brown/Mr. Wallace Wilder Dr. Phyllis Physician and Mr. Fred Herman For more than two: Mr. T. T. Jones, Ms. L. C. White, Ms. M. K. duPont or on one line each

Here's a list of other courtesy titles and how to write them:

Attorney:	Jane R. Blake, Esquire (or Esq. or J.D.) Ms. Jane R. Blake, Attorney at Law
State Attorney, Judge, Mayor, Governor, Cabinet Member, Congressperson, Senator, Representative:	The Honorable J. J. Jay
President:	The President
General:	General (or Gen.) George Patton, USAF (USMC, USN, etc.)

Ambassador:	The Honorable J. J. Jay (or American Ambassador to Mexico Ambassador)
	Her Excellency Juanita Rodriguez (or Mexican Ambassador to the U.S. Ambassador)
Chief Justice:	The Chief Justice of the United States
Consul, Consul General, Vice Consul:	Mr. William Stick, Esq. American Consul Paris, France
	The Honorable Chu Sumu Chinese Consul Washington, DC 20001
Professor:	Professor A. B. Galen, PhD Dr. A. B. Galen
Minister:	The Reverend Billy Graham The Reverend Dr. Graham
Priest:	The Reverend Graham Thomas The Reverend Dr. Thomas The Reverend Father Graham Thomas The Reverend Father Thomas
Rabbi:	Rabbi Jacob Stein
Cardinal in the U.S.:	His Eminence Emanuel Syne His Eminence Cardinal Syne
Mother Superior:	The Reverend Mother Superior Reverend Mother Mary Jane Smith Mother Mary Jane Smith, Superior
Sister:	Sister Mary Jane Smith, RSCJ Sister Mary Jane Smith, SC

*See Page 105 for proper salutation forms.

BUSINESS CORRESPONDENCE (Continued)

Names

People value their names, so watch the spelling. If you were soliciting my business or my attendance at your function and you misspelled my name after having seen it, I would not be as likely to accommodate you.

Of course there are times when you can't be certain about the spelling. If you don't have a definite spelling, call and ask. It may not be feasible to make a long distance call, but you can always make a local call. If you can't find out for certain, be very careful in your guessing.

Never address a letter to a woman using her husband's first name. Her first name is hers. Also, if she has retained her maiden name, use it even if you know her married name, and it's especially important to use *Ms.* in this case.

If you're writing to a particular person in a company but you don't know a name and are forced to address the letter to, for instance, *Personnel Manager,* that title takes the place of a name. Of course you can telephone a local company to get the person's name. It only takes a minute or two to call, and people will pay more attention to a letter addressed personally to them.

Business Titles

In a business letter, a title (such as *Secretary of State* or *Purchasing Director*) goes underneath the person's name, unless it is very short (like *Director* or *President*), in which case it goes after the person's name on the same line. You may also place it before the company name on *that* line. In these instances, always separate the title from the name with a comma, and never abbreviate. (You may abbreviate if the title is very long and on a line by itself.) Where to type the title is strictly a matter of the most well-balanced arrangement. If a person holds two offices, use the higher title.

Company Names

Be careful to type the name of the company correctly and use the entire name. In *The XYZ Company Incorporated,* be sure to include and capitalize *The,* and spell out *Incorporated.* For *Sears and Roebuck,* check the letterhead or phone book to find out if they use an ampersand (&) or *and.* Spell out the words *Company, Incorporated, Corporation,* and *Limited* unless the company itself abbreviates. Many corporations are now omitting the comma before *Inc.* If they do, honor their styling.

Departments

Spell out the name of the department and position it below the company name. You don't need to list both a full business title (Accounting Manager) and a corresponding department (Accounting Department).

Addresses

The best place to get the correct mailing address is from the addressee's own correspondence. If they have a post office box, use that instead of the street address. It's easier and faster to type, and it will be delivered quicker. You don't need to write out *Post Office Box* and *"PO"* doesn't need periods or spaces. Use the street address for mail that must be signed for or delivered, and when there is no box number.

Use numerals in the street address—except *One,* which should be spelled out. Write out streets named *First* through *Twelfth,* but use Arabic numbers for any street number after *Twelfth.* If a numbered street over *Twelfth* follows a house number with no words in between, insert a spaced hyphen between them (13 - 13th Street).

Spell out *Street* and other variations, such as *Parkway* or *Avenue,* in the inside address. You may always abbreviate *Boulevard.*

There is usually a comma between the street name and any directional letters (NW, SE). Always capitalize directional letters. The periods are seldom used, and there are no spaces between the letters. If the directional word comes *before* the street, write it out (East 57th Street).

If the company has a suite number, put it on the same line as the street address, with either a comma or two spaces between. Write out the word *Suite.* If it's too long to go on the same line, place it by itself on the line *above.*

Below the street address comes the city and state. You may abbreviate the name of the state with the proper two-letter abbreviations (all caps no period). If you do write out the state, be sure you have enough *s*'s and *p*'s in *Mississippi,* and remember to put an *s* on *Illinois* and an *h* on *Pittsburgh* and verify any other tricky spellings.

The ZIP code has become very important in addresses since our postal system has become computerized. Even if your letter says *Hartford, CT,* it could end up in Hawaii if it has Hawaii's ZIP code on it. Get a current ZIP code book (available from the post office) and take the time to use it.

BUSINESS CORRESPONDENCE (Continued)

THE SALUTATION

Place the salutation two to four lines beneath the city/state or attention line, flush with the left margin. Always use a colon on a typed letter, a comma on a handwritten letter.

The only courtesy titles normally abbreviated in the salutation are *Dr., Mr., Messrs., Mrs., Mmes., Ms., Mses., Msses.* Write out the others, even if you abbreviated in the inside address.

If you're writing to one of those imaginary people who run departments but don't have a name, it's usually best to say *Dear Personnel Manager* (or whatever). *Dear Sir or Madam* is acceptable, but most women bristle at *Madam,* and *Sir* seems haughty. If you're writing to the company itself, it's usually *Ladies and Gentlemen* (unless, of course, you're writing to an organization that is strictly female or male). You may also say *Dear Crisp Publications.*

If you have used an attention line, the letter is formally addressed to the company, so the salutation is to the company: *Ladies and Gentlemen.*

If, for some reason, you wish to say more than just *Dear,* as in *My dear Mr. Fraser, dear* is not capitalized.

The proper salutation for a letter not addressed to any particular person or company, such as a letter of recommendation, is *To Whom It May Concern.* Remember that there is no complimentary close when this salutation is used.

The facing page contains some helpful guidelines for salutations.

SALUTATIONS

Two men:	Gentlemen Dear Messrs. Jones and Smith Dear Mr. Smith and Mr. Jones
Two Women: **Married:**	Dear Mesdames (or Mmes.) Jones and Smith (or separate names with *Mrs.*)
Single:	Dear Misses (or Msses.) Jones and Smith (or separate names with *Miss*)
In general:	Dear Mses. Jones and Smith (or separate names with *Ms.*)
Man/Woman with different names:	Dear Ms. Bowen and Mr. Fanchot
One holds title:	Dear Judge Smith and Mr. Jones Dear Dr. and Mrs. (or Mr.) Smith
Doctor:	Dear Doctor (or Dr.) Smith
Attorney:	Dear Ms. Blake (*'Esq.'* is never used in a salutation)
Judge:	Dear Judge Jay
Chief Justice:	Dear Madam (or Mr.) Chief Justice
Mayor:	Dear Mayor Johnson *or* Dear Mr. (or Ms.) Mayor
Governor:	Dear Governor Wilcox
Cabinet member:	Dear Ms. (or Mr.) Secretary
Congressperson:	Dear Congressperson Smith Dear Ms. (or Mr.) Smith
Senator:	Dear Senator Goldstein
President:	Dear Mr. President *or* Dear President Bush
General:	Dear General (or Gen.) Patton
Ambassador:	Dear Mr. (or Madam) Ambassador Dear Ambassador Black
Consul, Consul General, Vice Consul:	Dear Ms. (or Mr.) Randall
Professor:	Dear Professor Lee
Clergy:	Dear Dr. (or Mr.) Lake *or* Dear Professor Tyler (*'The Reverend'* or *'Reverend'* are not used in business salutations)
Priest:	Dear Father Graham
Rabbi:	Dear Rabbi Stein
Cardinal the U.S.:	Your Eminence *or* Dear Cardinal Sheenan
Mother Superior:	Dear Reverend Mother Dear Reverend Mother Mary Smith
Sister:	Dear Sister *or* Dear Sister Mary Angelica

BUSINESS CORRESPONDENCE (Continued)

THE SIGNATURE BLOCK

Complimentary Close

Place the closing two lines below the last line of the body. In a block-style letter, the close is flush left. Only the first word of the complimentary close is capitalized. A comma follows the closing word in both typed and handwritten letters.

The most common closings in modern business correspondence are *Sincerely* and *Cordially*. Most writers have dropped the *yours* from these closings because it has no real meaning. Such closings as *Regards* and *Cordially* should be saved for people with whom the writer is on a first-name basis.

At one time, expressions like *I remain* and *I am* were used before, not in place of, complimentary closings, but they are considered too formal today. *With best wishes,* however, is still an acceptable expression *before* the complimentary close, and the shorter *Best wishes* may *replace* the closing.

Your Name

In a business letter, type your name four to six lines (leave enough room for your signature) beneath the close, always aligned directly beneath the close. (If your name is long enough to overrun the right margin, you may *center* it beneath the complimentary close.) Capitalize only the first letter of each element of the name, and only the first letter of each major element of the business title and/or department name (which go directly under the signature) if they are included in a business letter. You may omit your business title and department name if they appear on the letterhead. You may also omit your name if it's the only one on the letterhead—unless your handwriting is illegible. Never use the name of the company in the signature block when using letterhead.

Include any academic degrees or professional designations after your surname so the recipient will know how to reply correctly, unless these designations are already included on the printed letterhead. Never use your degrees in the written signature.

You needn't include a courtesy title in the signature line, unless your name could belong to either a male or a female, or if you want a courtesy title specified (if, for instance, you prefer to be called *Mrs.* instead of *Ms.*). When this is the case, place the courtesy title before your typewritten name, usually in parentheses: *(Mrs.) Marsha Mallone.*

THE SIGNATURE BLOCK

If you sign a letter for someone else, put your initials immediately below and to the right of the writer's surname, or center them under the full name. The words *Dictated but not read* are not necessary; your initials indicate that you've been instructed to sign the letter. If you're writing under your own name and want the recipient to know your title, indicate it as *Assistant to Mrs. Baucraft,* using only your manager's courtesy title and surname.

Copy Notations

A copy notation, now referred to as a courtesy copy, is placed at the left margin, two lines below the last notation. You may use *Copy, Copies to:, cc, cc:, C:, c,* or just about any other form.

List multiple recipients of copies alphabetically, even if you show only their initials. If you use only surnames, always use courtesy titles. If you show first names or initials along with the last names, you may omit courtesy titles.

Postscripts

Although many writers use them for emphasis, postscripts are not recommended for business correspondence. If you do use a postscript, place it two to four lines beneath the last notation. If your letter is block style, the P.S. is also blocked; if your paragraphs are indented, the first line of the P.S. is also indented. It is not necessary to begin a postscript with the initials *P.S.* A postscript should always be initialed by the writer.

EXERCISE

Answer *true* or *false*. For those you answer false, what *is* the correct answer?

True	False	
☐	☐	1. The correct order in which the bottom lines on a letter should be typed is: complimentary close, signature, typist's initials, enclosures, mailing instructions, and copy notations.
☐	☐	2. Your state senator is addressed as ''The Honorable Mr. Dinkelstaat'' in an inside address.
☐	☐	3. ''Respectfully yours'' is the best complimentary close to use in business letters.
☐	☐	4. A woman should always be addressed with her husband's name (Mrs. John Smith).
☐	☐	5. You should use a courtesy title in your handwritten signature.
☐	☐	6. In a typed letter, you may use a title like ''Esq.,'' ''M.D.,'' or ''C.P.S.,'' in the handwritten signature.
☐	☐	7. If your name is the only name on the letterhead, you may omit it beneath your signature.
☐	☐	8. There's no difference between the styling of business letters and personal letters.
☐	☐	9. The name of your company should always be typed two lines beneath the complimentary close.
☐	☐	10. If you have a business title and a department for your addressee, you need to use both of them in the inside address.

Answers on page 116

S E C T I O N

IX

Summary and
Answers to
Exercises

SUMMARY AND
ANSWERS

ETIQUOTE
Work spares us from three great evils: boredom, vice, and need.

—Voltaire,
Candide

SUMMARY

One way to become what you want to be, whatever you choose, is to study the people who *are* that way. About ten years ago, I became dissatisfied with my lifestyle. I was not very professional or successful (in my eyes, at least). My mother—who's a very wise woman—said, ''Kay, if you want to be successful, you have to hang around with successful people.'' So I began to associate with and study people who were strong, who were successful. I wanted to know what made them that way.

You can do the same thing. If you know someone who is professional, someone who is tactfully assertive, someone who has the attributes, characteristics, skills, and good manners described in this book, study that person. When you see people you think are really top-notch, get to know those people. Watch what they do—how they act. Ask yourself, ''What clothing do they have on, how do they walk, how do they talk, what is their voice like, what did they just say or do that intimidated or impressed me?'' You can start your learning process just by imitating those you respect.

But please don't take these rules of business etiquette (or any other social *rules*) *too* seriously. Socializing with others—like life itself—is supposed to be enjoyable. Enjoyment is extremely important to your professional life, your personal life, and your career success.

Research at major universities has identified several characteristics associated with high achievers—people who get the things they want. These are happy and balanced in their mental, emotional, physical, financial, and spiritual lives. They continuously focus on, review, and refine the habits of their mind, body, and emotions. They believe in both a higher being and a higher self. They possess a perspective and a sense of purpose that are not limited by time and space and ''what used to be'' or ''what should be.'' With this dignified sense of self-worth blended with balance and purpose, hard work and commitment, respect and kindness for others, these people achieve extraordinary things. But they are only ordinary people. . .just like you.

Good luck!

Kay

ANSWERS TO EXERCISE QUESTIONS

SECTION II (page 18)

1. False. Change the subject or say, without sarcasm, "I'd rather not discuss my personal life. You don't mind, do you?"

2. False. Never make passes at coworkers, don't pay personal compliments to strangers, and never berate your own company—no matter how long you've been there.

3. False. Accept the gift graciously, even if you didn't really need (or want) the favor.

4. False. Never discuss anything confidential with your coworkers.

5. False. Coming to work late shows a lack of commitment and dedication; working through lunch shows that you weren't hungry.

6. False. You never get a second chance to make a first impression.

7. False. It's a two-way street and each side has total responsibility for the communication.

8. False. Be even *more* reserved in the beginning. Give them time to get used to your presence before you start being the office charmer.

9. False. Most managers prefer to hear solutions, not problems. No one minds answering your questions in the beginning, or even helping you solve a few minor problems, but don't expect that help to last forever.

10. False. It's up to *you* to make you—and them—feel comfortable. Go out of your way to meet your new coworkers and make friends.

SECTION III (pages 33-34)

1. (B) Shake, but apologize for your hands, explaining that you've been drinking a cold drink.

2. (B) Ask again, because you don't want to alienate a potential associate.

3. (B) Stand up and offer your hand.

4. (A) Rise and greet her if it's an unusual occasion or if she is much higher in rank; *or* (C) Look up and greet her if it's a common occurrence.

5. (B) Tell the visitor that you'll tell the owner he is there, but only if you can tell her the nature of his business.

6. (A) The client's name.

7. *Yes.* It's always appropriate for a man—or a woman—to initiate a handshake.

8. Repeat the name immediately and then to yourself several times. Associate the name and/or person with the person's hobbies or interests or career.

9. Admit it or make a humorous statement about it.

10. Ten minutes.

ANSWERS TO EXERCISE QUESTIONS

SECTION IV (page 46)

Scoring

Give yourself 4 points for *Always* answers; 2 points for *Usually*; 0 points for *Seldom*.

64–56 points: You have a winning telephone personality!
55–46 points: A little more effort will bring big rewards!
Below 46: Concentrate on forming better telephone habits and try this test again.

SECTION V (page 63)

1. False. The site should be determined by the theme and purpose of the meeting.

2. False. Stand out of respect, especially when the woman is a higher-ranking person, a guest, or an older person.

3. False. It's better etiquette to separate them.

4. False. They need at least 48 hours, preferably a week.

5. True.

6. False. That's one of the duties of a receptionist. He or she is not there to wait on you or keep you company, however.

7. False. Wait for your host to indicate which seat you should take.

8. False. Keep your papers in your lap.

9. False. Always choose a conservative style unless you are interviewing for a creative position.

10. False. *Never* smoke in an interviewer's office, even if they do.

11. False. Just keep them nonpersonal and not totally centered around you and your benefits.

SECTION VI (page 80)

1. False. You may order a drink (preferably wine or beer, and only one) if you want it, but not for that reason. And it's certainly all right to decline. It may even be *better* to order something soft, since you *are* representing both your company and your manager.

2. False. Wineglasses should be held by the stem, not the bowl.

3. False. It's quite acceptable if your drink is very hot.

4. False. The highest-ranking person goes on your right.

5. False. Wait in the lobby if possible. If there is no lobby, you may wait at the bar or at your table.

6. False. The host always pays (even if the host is a hostess).

7. False. The host immediately follows the maitre d', with the guest in the rear.

8. False. Always serve your guests first.

9. False. Tipping should be for good service. If the service was poor, the tip should be poor—or nonexistent.

10. False. Both may be eaten whole from your fork.

SECTION VII (page 93)

1. True, although it's still a thoughtful gesture.

2. False. Men like flowers too!

3. False. You may return it to the store for replacement or exchange or you may return it to the giver if you think it would be inappropriate to keep it.

4. False. Even close friends deserve courtesy.

5. False. A clock denotes death to the Japanese people.

6. False. Thank-you notes are essential to good etiquette.

7. False, especially if your meal function was for business reasons.

8. False. It means, ''Let us know either way.''

9. True. Or they may be engraved.

10. False. Although it's safe and easy, it's often considered impersonal by the recipient.

SECTION VII (page 108)

1. False. Mailing instructions are typed beneath the date, wherever it's placed.

2. True.

3. False. Never use this closing except in the most formal reports, minutes, and legal documents.

4. False. Never address a woman this way unless she specifically requests it.

5. False. You may use a courtesy title in your *typewritten* signature if you want to specify your gender, but never in your handwritten signature.

6. False. The reverse is true; use your title in the *typewritten,* but not the handwritten signature.

7. True.

8. False. See Figure 5.

9. False. If your company name appears on the letterhead, do not repeat it in the close.

10. False. They are often redundant—for example, ''Marketing Director, Marketing Department.''

YE OLDE OFFICE RULES*

Working conditions have changed quite a bit over the past 100 years. Just read over these office regulations for a New Jersey carriage manufacturing firm in 1872:

I. Employees will daily sweep floors and dust the furniture.

II. Each day employees will fill lamps, clean chimneys, and trim wicks.

III. Each clerk will bring in a bucket of water and a scuttle of coal for the day's business.

IV. Employees will make their pens carefully. Nibs may be whittled to individual tastes.

V. The office will open at 7:00 a.m. and close at 8:00 p.m. daily, except on the Sabbath on which day it remains closed.

VI. Men employees will be given an evening off each week for courting purposes, or two evenings a week if they go regularly to church.

VII. After an employee has passed his hours of labor in the office, he should spend the time reading the Bible and other good books.

VIII. Every employee should lay aside from each pay a goodly sum of his earnings for his benefit during his declining years so that he will not become a burden on the charity of others.

IX. Any employee who smokes Spanish cigars, uses liquor in any form, or frequents pool and public halls will give me good reason to suspect his worth, intentions, integrity, and honesty.

X. The employee who has performed his labors faithfully and without fault for a period of five years and who has been thrifty and attentive to his religious duties will be given an increase of five cents per day, providing a just return in profit from the business permits.

*AUTHOR UNKNOWN

NOTES

FOR OTHER FIFTY-MINUTE SELF-STUDY BOOKS
SEE ORDER FORM AT THE BACK OF THE BOOK.

THE FIFTY-MINUTE SERIES

Quantity	Title	Code #	Price	Amount
	MANAGEMENT TRAINING			
	Self-Managing Teams	000-0	$7.95	
	Delegating For Results	008-6	$7.95	
	Successful Negotiation—Revised	09-2	$7.95	
	Increasing Employee Productivity	010-8	$7.95	
	Personal Performance Contracts—Revised	12-2	$7.95	
	Team Building—Revised	16-5	$7.95	
	Effective Meeting Skills	33-5	$7.95	
	An Honest Day's Work: Motivating Employees To Excel	39-4	$7.95	
	Managing Disagreement Constructively	41-6	$7.95	
	Training Managers To Train	43-2	$7.95	
	Learning To Lead	043-4	$7.95	
	The Fifty-Minute Supervisor—Revised	58-0	$7.95	
	Leadership Skills For Women	62-9	$7.95	
	Systematic Problem Solving & Decision Making	63-7	$7.95	
	Coaching & Counseling	68-8	$7.95	
	Ethics In Business	69-6	$7.95	
	Understanding Organizational Change	71-8	$7.95	
	Project Management	75-0	$7.95	
	Risk Taking	76-9	$7.95	
	Managing Organizational Change	80-7	$7.95	
	Working Together In A Multi-Cultural Organization	85-8	$7.95	
	Selecting And Working With Consultants	87-4	$7.95	
	PERSONNEL MANAGEMENT			
	Your First Thirty Days: A Professional Image in a New Job	003-5	$7.95	
	Office Management: A Guide To Productivity	005-1	$7.95	
	Men and Women: Partners at Work	009-4	$7.95	
	Effective Performance Appraisals—Revised	11-4	$7.95	
	Quality Interviewing—Revised	13-0	$7.95	
	Personal Counseling	14-9	$7.95	
	Attacking Absenteeism	042-6	$7.95	
	New Employee Orientation	46-7	$7.95	
	Professional Excellence For Secretaries	52-1	$7.95	
	Guide To Affirmative Action	54-8	$7.95	
	Writing A Human Resources Manual	70-X	$7.95	
	Winning at Human Relations	86-6	$7.95	
	WELLNESS			
	Mental Fitness	15-7	$7.95	
	Wellness in the Workplace	020-5	$7.95	
	Personal Wellness	021-3	$7.95	

THE FIFTY-MINUTE SERIES (Continued)

Quantity	Title	Code #	Price	Amount
	WELLNESS (CONTINUED)			
	Preventing Job Burnout	23-8	$7.95	
	Job Performance and Chemical Dependency	27-0	$7.95	
	Overcoming Anxiety	029-9	$7.95	
	Productivity at the Workstation	041-8	$7.95	
	COMMUNICATIONS			
	Technical Writing In The Corporate World	004-3	$7.95	
	Giving and Receiving Criticism	023-X	$7.95	
	Effective Presentation Skills	24-6	$7.95	
	Better Business Writing—Revised	25-4	$7.95	
	Business Etiquette And Professionalism	032-9	$7.95	
	The Business Of Listening	34-3	$7.95	
	Writing Fitness	35-1	$7.95	
	The Art Of Communicating	45-9	$7.95	
	Technical Presentation Skills	55-6	$7.95	
	Making Humor Work	61-0	$7.95	
	Visual Aids In Business	77-7	$7.95	
	Speed-Reading In Business	78-5	$7.95	
	Publicity Power	82-3	$7.95	
	Influencing Others	84-X	$7.95	
	SELF-MANAGEMENT			
	Attitude: Your Most Priceless Possession-Revised	011-6	$7.95	
	Personal Time Management	22-X	$7.95	
	Successful Self-Management	26-2	$7.95	
	Balancing Home And Career—Revised	035-3	$7.95	
	Developing Positive Assertiveness	38-6	$7.95	
	The Telephone And Time Management	53-X	$7.95	
	Memory Skills In Business	56-4	$7.95	
	Developing Self-Esteem	66-1	$7.95	
	Creativity In Business	67-X	$7.95	
	Managing Personal Change	74-2	$7.95	
	Stop Procrastinating: Get To Work!	88-2	$7.95	
	CUSTOMER SERVICE/SALES TRAINING			
	Sales Training Basics—Revised	02-5	$7.95	
	Restaurant Server's Guide—Revised	08-4	$7.95	
	Telephone Courtesy And Customer Service	18-1	$7.95	
	Effective Sales Management	031-0	$7.95	
	Professional Selling	42-4	$7.95	
	Customer Satisfaction	57-2	$7.95	
	Telemarketing Basics	60-2	$7.95	
	Calming Upset Customers	65-3	$7.95	
	Quality At Work	72-6	$7.95	
	Managing Quality Customer Service	83-1	$7.95	
	Quality Customer Service—Revised	95-5	$7.95	
	SMALL BUSINESS AND FINANCIAL PLANNING			
	Understanding Financial Statements	022-1	$7.95	
	Marketing Your Consulting Or Professional Services	40-8	$7.95	

THE FIFTY-MINUTE SERIES (Continued)

Quantity	Title	Code #	Price	Amount
	SMALL BUSINESS AND FINANCIAL PLANNING (CONTINUED)			
	Starting Your New Business	44-0	$7.95	
	Personal Financial Fitness — Revised	89-0	$7.95	
	Financial Planning With Employee Benefits	90-4	$7.95	
	BASIC LEARNING SKILLS			
	Returning To Learning: Getting Your G.E.D.	002-7	$7.95	
	Study Skills Strategies — Revised	05-X	$7.95	
	The College Experience	007-8	$7.95	
	Basic Business Math	024-8	$7.95	
	Becoming An Effective Tutor	028-0	$7.95	
	CAREER PLANNING			
	Career Discovery	07-6	$7.95	
	Effective Networking	030-2	$7.95	
	Preparing for Your Interview	033-7	$7.95	
	Plan B: Protecting Your Career	48-3	$7.95	
	I Got the Job!	59-9	$7.95	
	RETIREMENT			
	Personal Financial Fitness — Revised	89-0	$7.95	
	Financial Planning With Employee Benefits	90-4	$7.95	

OTHER CRISP INC. BOOKS

Quantity	Title	Code #	Price	Amount
	Desktop Publishing	001-9	$ 5.95	
	Stepping Up To Supervisor	11-8	$13.95	
	The Unfinished Business Of Living: Helping Aging Parents	19-X	$12.95	
	Managing Performance	23-7	$19.95	
	Be True To Your Future: A Guide To Life Planning	47-5	$13.95	
	Up Your Productivity	49-1	$10.95	
	Comfort Zones: Planning Your Future 2/e	73-4	$13.95	
	Copyediting 2/e	94-7	$18.95	
	Recharge Your Career	027-2	$12.95	
	Practical Time Management	275-4	$13.95	

VIDEO TITLE*

Quantity	Video Title*	Code #	Preview	Purchase	Amount
	Attitude: Your Most Priceless Possession	012-4	$25.00	$395.00	
	Quality Customer Service	013-2	$25.00	$395.00	
	Team Building	014-2	$25.00	$395.00	
	Job Performance & Chemical Dependency	015-9	$25.00	$395.00	
	Better Business Writing	016-7	$25.00	$395.00	
	Comfort Zones	025-6	$25.00	$395.00	
	Creativity in Business	036-1	$25.00	$395.00	
	Motivating at Work	037-X	$25.00	$395.00	
	Calming Upset Customers	040-X	$25.00	$395.00	
	Balancing Home and Career	048-5	$25.00	$395.00	
	Stress and Mental Fitness	049-3	$25.00	$395.00	

(*Note: All tapes are VHS format. Video package includes five books and a Leader's Guide.)

THE FIFTY-MINUTE SERIES
(Continued)

	Amount
Total Books	
Less Discount (5 or more different books 20% sampler)	
Total Videos	
Less Discount (purchase of 3 or more videos earn 20%)	
Shipping ($3.50 per video, $.50 per book)	
California Tax (California residents add 7%)	
TOTAL	

☐ Send volume discount information.   ☐ Mastercard ☐ VISA ☐ AMEX

☐ Please send me a catalog.   Exp. Date _____

Account No. _____   Name (as appears on card) _____

Ship to: _____   Bill to: _____

_____   _____

_____   _____

_____   _____

Phone number: _____   P.O. # _____

All orders except those with a P.O.# must be prepaid.
For more information Call (415) 949-4888 or FAX (415) 949-1610.